New Entrepreneurs and High Performance Enterprises in the Middle East and North Africa

BETTER POLICIES FOR BETTER LIVES

International Development Research Centre
Centre de recherches pour le développement international

This work is published on the responsibility of the Secretary-General of the OECD. The opinions expressed and arguments employed herein do not necessarily reflect the official views of the Organisation or the views of Canada's International Development Research Centre or the members of its board of governors.

This document and any map included herein are without prejudice to the status of or sovereignty over any territory, to the delimitation of international frontiers and boundaries and to the name of any territory, city or area.

ISBN 978-92-64-10025-1 (print)
ISBN 978-92-64-17919-6 (PDF)

Series: Competitiveness and Private Sector Development
ISSN 2076-5754 (print)
ISSN 2076-5762 (online)

http://dx.doi.org/10.1787/9789264179196-en

The statistical data for Israel are supplied by and under the responsibility of the relevant Israeli authorities. The use of such data by the OECD is without prejudice to the status of the Golan Heights, East Jerusalem and Israeli settlements in the West Bank under the terms of international law.

Photo credits: Cover © Fotolia/MON.

Corrigenda to OECD publications may be found on line at: *www.oecd.org/publishing/corrigenda*.

Foreword

A growing body of research points to the important role of high growth enterprises in employment creation, productivity and economic growth. Most of the literature, however, focuses on OECD countries and a few emerging economies, and evidence for the Middle East and North Africa (MENA) region remains limited. This study addresses this information gap by focusing on young and high growth enterprises in the MENA region as important drivers of change, job creation and stronger competition.

While there has been a significant increase in the general level of education and the number of young graduates across the MENA region during the last decade, evidence suggests that few of them aspire to become entrepreneurs. Instead, most seek work in the public sector or in large companies. This illustrates the need for a better understanding of the enterprise-creation process in the region and greater knowledge of personal motivations, objectives, incentives and disincentives, and external factors. Recognising this challenge, the MENA-OECD Working Group on SME Policy, Entrepreneurship and Human Capital Development proposed to conduct analysis of new entrepreneurship in the region on the occasion of its Tunis meeting held in March 2010.*

The report New Entrepreneurs and High Growth Enterprises in the MENA Region analyses the challenges and opportunities facing young enterprises and their owners throughout the MENA region. It provides a balanced review of the arguments for and against an active government policy supporting high growth enterprises, drawing on evidence and experience from OECD countries. New Entrepreneurs offers a number of policy recommendations to support the creation of high growth and future high-impact firms with the potential to make a dynamic contribution to job creation and economic growth. Finally, the report recognises that policy initiatives in favour of enterprise creation depend on the specific circumstances and capacities of individual governments. Constant evaluation of new and existing policies is a key ingredient of success.

The report is the result of the partnership between the OECD and Canada's International Development Research Centre (IDRC), which has extensive knowledge of entrepreneurship and SME policy issues as well as a network of researchers and experts across the MENA region. It reflects the contributions of a team of researchers, experts and editors from the MENA region and OECD countries, including the Secretariat of the OECD Private Sector Development Division and the IDRC.

New Entrepreneurs makes use of the Global Entrepreneurship Monitor (GEM) database, including information on the MENA region. The report complements this data with insights into the enterprise-creation process and early years of trading gathered from interviews with entrepreneurs

---

* The Working Group, established in 2008 in the framework of the MENA-OECD Investment Programme, brings together policy makers, representatives of private sector associations, SME experts, representatives of international organisations and donors, to discuss entrepreneurship and SME development, exchange experiences and elaborate policy guidelines. The MENA-OECD Investment Programme is supported by voluntary contributions from Sweden, the United States, Japan, Turkey, Czech Republic, the United Kingdom, Spain, Germany and the European Commission.

running young businesses. The insights provide a qualitative perspective on the statistical analysis and help formulate policy recommendations.

This study breaks new ground in understanding the dynamics of enterprise creation and sustainability in the MENA region. It is hoped that it will contribute to the search for stable and prosperous societies in the region.

Acknowledgements

The publication is produced by the MENA-OECD Investment Programme. The International Development Research Centre (IDRC) contributed financially to the preparation of the study and the case studies that informed the analysis. The report was prepared by Professor David Storey, School of Business, Management and Economics, University of Sussex, United Kingdom; and by the Secretariat of the MENA-OECD Investment Programme, including Antonio Fanelli and Jorge Gálvez Méndez.

Chapter 2 draws extensively on the working paper published in 2013 (forthcoming) by the OECD and IDRC, *Firm Creation in the Business Life Course: MENA Countries in the Global Context*, by Professor Paul Reynolds, Research Professor of Management, George Washington University, United States.

The case studies of high growth enterprises were undertaken by: Dr. Hala Hattab, Lecturer in Business Administration, The British University in Egypt; Mr. Mohamed Dahshan, Government Policy Consultant, Egypt; Dr. Dale Murphy, Director of Entrepreneurship, Dubai School of Government, UAE; Mr. Mohammed Derrabi, Vice President for Academic Affairs, Université Internationale de Rabat, Morocco; Mr. Faysal Mansouri, Team Leader, General Coordinator, Global Entrepreneurship Monitor, University of Sousse, Tunisia; and Professor Ghassan Omet, Assistant Professor, Finance, The University of Jordan.

The editorial team included Susan Joekes and Martha Melesse (IDRC), as well as Antonio Fanelli, Jorge Gálvez Méndez, Vanessa Vallée, Yvonne Giesing, Korin Kane and Emma Beer from the OECD. Comments were provided by Anthony O'Sullivan, Alexander Böhmer, Nicola Ehlermann-Cache, Ania Thiemann and Vanessa Vallée (OECD) as well as Lois Stevenson (former Research Fellow at IDRC, Cairo), Martha Melesse, Edgar Rodriguez and Arjan de Haan (IDRC). The study was edited by Colm Foy, Consultant, former Co-ordinator, Black Sea and Central Asia Initiative, OECD Development Centre.

Table of contents

Figures

Acronyms and glossary of terms

EGP	Egyptian Pound
EIP	OECD-Eurostat Entrepreneurship Indicators Programme
GDP	Gross Domestic Product
GEM	Global Entrepreneurship Monitor
GII	Global Innovation Index
High growth enterprise	As measured by employment (or turnover), are firms with average annualised growth in employees (or in turnover) greater than 20% a year, over a three-year period, and with ten or more employees at the beginning of the observation period.
High potential enterprise	An enterprise with potential to become high growth based on four proxy indicators: if it operates in a sector likely to employ staff with comparatively higher technical skills; firms which are expecting an impact in their markets; firms expecting growth in employment; and firms with 25% or more of their customers residing in foreign markets.
ICT	Information and Communication Technology
IDI	ICT Development Index
IDRC	International Development Research Centre
IMC	Industrial Modernisation Centre
LLC	Limited Liability Corporation
MBA	Master of Business Administration
MENA	Middle East and North Africa
NILEX	Nile Stock Exchange
OECD	Organisation for Economic Co-operation and Development
OPIC	Overseas Private Investment Corporation
PLC	Public Limited Company
PPP	Purchasing Power Parity
SBA	The United States Small Business Administration
SICAR	Risk Capital Investment Society (Société d'Investissement à Capital Risque)
SME	Small and medium-sized enterprises
R&D	Research and Development
WPSMEE	OECD Working Party on SMEs and Entrepreneurship

Executive summary

The economic growth and job creation challenge for the MENA region

One of the most significant challenges facing the Middle East and North Africa (MENA) is the creation of economic opportunities and jobs to reduce the high levels of unemployment and absorb the growing number of people entering the labour force.

The job challenge is even more pressing in the current context of transition and reform. The lack of social and economic equity was one of the main catalysts of the wave of protests that swept the region in 2011 and led to the dismissal of longstanding regimes in some countries. The slow-down of economic activity and postponement and cancellation of investment projects in several countries has put further pressure on MENA economies to respond to increasing demands and expectations.

Promoting entrepreneurship and the development of high growth enterprises to address the challenge

To meet this challenge, MENA economies need to boost economic growth, and provide more and better opportunities for their increasingly educated young generations. The promotion of entrepreneurship and small and medium-size enterprise (SME) growth is one of the most important means to achieve this, given their role as drivers of economic activity and growth.

SMEs constitute not only the vast majority of firms in all countries but also account for an important share of employment and, to varying degrees, value added and exports, among other economic and social contributions. Higher levels of enterprise creation, growth and exit are also closely linked to economic dynamism and the introduction of innovative products and production processes that can increase productivity and generate employment, both directly and indirectly through spillovers.

Therefore, finding ways to stimulate enterprise creation in the region is fundamental, especially for those types of firms that can make the strongest contribution to economic growth and job generation. This report focuses on high growth enterprises, defined as those growing 20% or more in terms of employment or turnover over a period of three or more consecutive years (according to the OECD-Eurostat definition). The report does not deny the importance of the majority of enterprises with lower or no growth, and of enterprises with decreasing and eventually disappearing activities. It rather highlights the relevance of the roughly 5% of enterprises that, by exploiting market opportunities, contribute to significant shares of new jobs (over 50%, according to some research), productivity, innovation and economic growth.

Evidence indicates that high growth is an event that can happen one or more times in the life of an enterprise; and is therefore not a permanent characteristic of any type of firm.

Research also shows that, while high growth is often correlated with innovation, many other factors can propel a firm's growth, such as a growing economy, the expansion of exports, an increase in government expenditure, and so on.

Because of their importance, high growth enterprises are increasingly attracting the attention of researchers and policy makers. Evidence, however, has been mostly developed for OECD countries and a few emerging economies, with very scant research in MENA. This report aims at advancing the knowledge on high growth enterprises in the region by addressing the following questions:

● Are MENA economies generating a significant pool of enterprises with the potential to become high growth? What are the characteristics of such enterprises vis-à-vis similar enterprises in developed and other emerging economies?

● What obstacles may prevent the pool of businesses with potential to become high growth enterprises from realising that potential? Is there evidence of an incoming generation of entrepreneurs with different profiles from incumbents in terms of education, motivations, professional experience and gender?

● Is the business environment conducive to high growth enterprises? What can public policy do to promote more such firms and what are MENA governments doing in this regard? What elements are still missing?

This report uses the Global Entrepreneurship Monitor (GEM) to provide quantitative information on the structure and characteristics of the enterprise population and on the profiles of enterprise owner-managers. The data allows for comparisons with developed and emerging economies. In-depth interviews with the graduate owner-managers of 20 current or potentially rapid-growth enterprises in Egypt, Jordan, Morocco, Tunisia and the UAE with fewer than six years of operation complement the data with qualitative information. The report also analyses the role of public policy in supporting high growth enterprises and reviews experience from the MENA region. It concludes with a number of policy implications.

The low levels of enterprise development and women's economic participation hold back the entrepreneurial potential in MENA

The MENA region is characterised by low levels of enterprise creation and development. According to data from the World Bank, only 0.6 new limited liability firms per 100 adults entered the economy in the MENA region during 2004-09, compared to over 4.2 in high-income countries, 2.2 in Europe and Central Asia and 1.3 in Latin America. This is confirmed by the GEM data used in this report. Even when considering both formal and informal enterprises, the MENA region lags behind other emerging economies: there are only 3.4 new formal and informal enterprises in MENA compared to nearly four in emerging Asia and over 4.6 in Latin America.

An important share of SMEs are characterised as informal or unregistered. Many small firms operate in low productivity sectors such as basic retailing, craft production, catering, and transport and are driven by necessity rather than economic opportunity. All these factors hinder the ability of SMEs and entrepreneurs to grow and generate higher quality jobs.

The low levels of participation of women in the economy further limit the economic growth and entrepreneurial potential of the MENA region. Only 32% of women of working age in MENA participate in the labour force, compared to 56% in low and middle-income countries and over 61% in OECD countries. The rate of self-employment for women is half that of men.

The relative share of firms with potential to become high growth in MENA is comparable to that of other emerging markets

This report finds that, despite their rarity, there are enterprises in MENA countries that correspond to the OECD-Eurostat high growth definition. Contrary to general perceptions, these enterprises are by no means exclusively operating in the high tech sectors. Instead, their exceptional performance often reflects their ability to identify new business opportunities and introduce innovative approaches to management and operations.

Proxy indicators used to evaluate the potential for the development of high growth firms in MENA suggest that the region registers comparable shares of high potential firms to other emerging economies. These indicators include the share of firms likely to employ staff with technical skills; firms expecting job growth; enterprises expecting to have an impact in the markets in which they operate; and enterprises with sales of 25% or more to foreign markets.

This, however, does not imply that there will be similar or higher numbers of high growth enterprises in MENA than in other regions. This is because MENA economies have lower levels of enterprise creation. In other words, if fewer firms are being created and developed then there will be a smaller population from which high growth enterprises (and all enterprises in general) are born.

Evidence also shows that the entrepreneurs behind high growth enterprises in MENA are often graduates with significant work experience, frequently driven by the pursuit of a business opportunity rather than economic necessity. Entrepreneurs leading nascent and infant enterprises (i.e. firms younger than 2.5 years) tend to have higher levels of education than those in other emerging economies. Information obtained from the case studies also suggests high-performance entrepreneurs are likely to have relevant and often diverse work experience.

An unfavourable business climate constrains the development of high growth firms

High growth enterprises are faced with barriers at two levels: wider factors negatively affecting the overall business climate and barriers that specifically limit their development.

A significant body of literature indicates that entrepreneurs and enterprises, including high growth ones, need a sound business environment in order to realise their job creation and economic growth potential. This includes the existence of efficient and unbiased market and political institutions to guarantee that the most competent and innovative entrepreneurs are able to compete on a level playing field and that well-connected enterprises do not exert undue influence in markets and distort competition. This also involves other important elements such as the existence of financial sectors responsive to the needs of SMEs and entrepreneurs, the availability of a sufficient and adequate set of skills in the labour force, and the existence of adequate infrastructure, among others.

However, it is often argued that the business environment in MENA countries tends to be less conducive to business creation and development than in developed and even in some emerging economies. Some studies have pointed to high levels of corruption, cumbersome regulatory frameworks, market dominance by a small group of well-connected and favoured firms, and a relatively generalised preference for employment in the public sector to the detriment of private enterprises. This has created a business environment that constrains private sector development, with an even more marked impact on SMEs.

It is also often argued that a small number of well-established enterprises in the region benefit disproportionately from strong market positions. This is the result of regulatory environments that restrict competition and of networks of business, financial and political interests with few incentives to innovate and drive change. In consequence, the total number of enterprises led by economic opportunity and operating formally in higher productivity sectors is smaller than in OECD countries and in dynamic emerging markets.

High growth enterprises also face specific barriers to their development

High growth enterprises face higher barriers to accessing finance than firms who have physical assets to offer as collateral. This includes both equity (business angels, seed funds, venture capital or equity funds) and bank credit in its various forms, including asset-based finance, term loans, overdrafts, overnight funding, leasing, factoring, hire-purchase and even personal credit cards.

The case studies show that entrepreneurial and managerial skills are a second challenge. Even though the owner-managers of high growth enterprises are well educated and have significant work experience, research shows that these entrepreneurs often lack the key skills needed to grow their businesses.

The low participation of women in the labour force is a major determinant of the entrepreneurial gender gap. Since women's reduced representation in the labour force as a whole deprives them of experience and training, they are less well equipped than their male peers to start a business.

Poor infrastructure services, including Internet and telecommunication services, poor road systems, unreliable electricity and inefficient water systems, strongly disadvantage high growth firms, who are often heavy users of these services.

Policy implications

To tackle these barriers effectively, two types of policy reforms are needed. The first involves improvements to the business environment; the second involves policies specifically targeted at high growth enterprises. These recommendations place the quality of the business environment at the heart of SME and entrepreneurship policy. By taking action in these areas, governments will send a strong signal to aspiring entrepreneurs that business creation is a viable alternative to other types of employment.

Key policy priorities for improved business environment include:

- A transparent regulatory framework through sound regulatory policy and regulatory simplification is necessary in order to increase competition. Governments need to pursue an active policy to remove obstacles to entry by creating a level playing field and fostering competition, particularly in sectors that present opportunities for growth. This requires a systematic review of the sector regulatory framework at national and local level, current competition, business and public procurement practices, rules and regulations governing professional bodies, and ensuring the enforcement of those rules. Unfair competition, either from the informal sector or from the abuse of dominant market positions, has to be eradicated. This alone will do most to transform marketplaces by creating conditions favourable for high growth and high potential enterprises, thereby boosting the wider performance of the MENA economies.

- Increased competition and diversification in the banking and financial sectors would help in ensuring that viable and promising businesses have better access to financing. Banks and financial institutions also need to develop adequate capabilities to better assess the business plans and projects of innovative and high potential enterprises.

- Policies to increase women's participation in the labour market and in enterprise creation are also key. Governments need to pursue gender policies including, among other things, support for women led enterprises and firms to hire qualified female interns/employees. This would give women relevant business training and experience outside the traditional sectors, opening up opportunities to develop a professional career or to start their own businesses.

- Legal and judiciary reform to improve contract enforcement could also increase the certainty of the business environment and foster risk taking.

- Human-capital development policies are important in order to improve skills and promote an entrepreneurial culture, including promoting the introduction of curricula on education and training for entrepreneurship at all educational levels.

To support high growth enterprises, MENA governments could focus their attention on the following priority areas:

- *Access to finance:* Several OECD governments, and the EU, have introduced programmes to stimulate private sector equity. Their experience could be informative for governments in the MENA region. To improve access to bank credit, which can be difficult to obtain, notably for high growth enterprises, governments need to ensure that financial institutions operate in competitive marketplaces. In addition, publicly funded credit agencies, present in most of the MENA countries, should introduce special schemes tailored to the needs of high growth enterprises.

- *Skills development including vocational training:* Governments in the MENA region need to give special attention to developing skills that are tailored to the needs of high growth enterprises. Examples of such customised programmes could include: voucher schemes that would allow specific types of enterprises to select trainers or advisors with part of the cost covered by public funds; joint development of internship programmes with universities and vocational institutes; and establishment of hiring programmes for new graduates, supported by tax credits or temporary government grants. Governments should encourage hiring students to work for periods of time in small and micro-enterprises. Such programmes can be mutually beneficial to both the student and the enterprise.

- There could also be a focus on strengthening *links between local high potential service enterprises and large enterprises*, including multinational firms (MNEs). This would not only be useful for fostering skills development in small and high growth enterprises but could also be instrumental in promoting certifications, quality improvements, etc.

Monitoring progress and testing new approaches

General measures aiming to improve the overall business environment would be beneficial for all types of enterprises. However, those measures can also be translated into more specific initiatives targeted to high growth enterprises. Pilot projects with clearly defined targets and objectives to identify effective ways to support the development of high growth enterprises could be undertaken. Careful monitoring and evaluation (and modification if necessary) of experimental policies will ensure their effectiveness and avoid any perception of preferential treatment of any particular enterprise group.

This type of approach implies the involvement of a wide range of actors, not least the business community and SME managers themselves. As such, economic reform in the region can contribute to building a more open society and helping promote more inclusive growth in the region.

These recommendations need to be complemented by further assessments and policy approaches tailored to the country specific context.

Chapter 1

Making the case
for high growth enterprises

This chapter documents the role of high growth enterprises in terms of employment, wealth creation and innovation. It draws upon studies in OECD and some emerging economies, as well as from the MENA region.

It notes the importance of enterprise births and deaths for job creation, loss and overall economic dynamism. The chapter includes analysis of the increasing importance of innovation from new and small firms. It further provides a characterisation of low growth and necessity-driven firms as well as high growth, innovative and opportunity-driven enterprises.

The MENA region faces daunting challenges for income and employment creation

Economies in the MENA region, especially those undergoing political transition and reform, face significant challenges, one of the most important of which is providing employment and economic opportunities for all segments of a growing population.

High levels of unemployment are partly due to a mismatch between job creation rates and the relatively high rates of economic growth and investment during the 2000s. The region has been characterised by low levels of enterprise creation, pervasive corruption, cumbersome business environments, large informal sectors, market dominance by a small group of well-connected and favoured firms, and a relatively generalised preference for employment in the public sector to the detriment of private enterprise (OECD-World Economic Forum, 2011).

This has resulted in an under-performing private sector, to the disadvantage particularly of young people, females and highly educated people. The 2011 events, leading to political and economic uncertainty, as well as weakened consumer and investor confidence, have further magnified the challenges faced by the region.

To spur job-rich growth, MENA economies need to restore investor and consumer confidence and further integrate into regional and global markets. They also need to foster homegrown sources of employment and income generation. One means of achieving this is to accelerate the creation and development of private enterprises, particularly small and medium-sized enterprises (SMEs).

The promotion of entrepreneurship and SME development is an important instrument to address the region's challenges

Small and medium-sized enterprises and entrepreneurs are widely recognised for their key role in wealth creation and employment. Despite the differences in definitions applied across different economies (Box 1.1), SMEs constitute the overwhelming majority of enterprises, account for important shares of total employment and contribute, to varying degrees, to total value added and exports. The annex to this chapter provides general facts and statistics about SMEs and entrepreneurship in OECD and MENA economies from different sources.

However, to capture fully the role of SMEs as engines of wealth and job creation requires a dynamic as well as a static perspective: what matters most for economic dynamism is not the number and size composition of firms *per se* but the rates of firm creation, survival, growth and exit, that is to say, *the entrepreneurial performance of economies.*[1]

Box 1.1. **Defining SMEs and entrepreneurship**

Governments adopt different definitions of micro, small and medium-sized enterprises depending on their specific socio-economic contexts and policy priorities. Most economies classify enterprises by size according to employment and/or turnover criteria, in some cases depending on the economic sector in which firms operate.

For instance, the European Commission, through Eurostat (its statistical office) defines SMEs as having between 1 and 249 persons employed, annual turnover of up to EUR 50 million and a balance sheet of no more than EUR 43 million. The United States Small Business Administration (SBA), for its part, classifies SMEs following industry-specific standards. In general, the SBA recognises a small business as having 500 or fewer employees and USD 7 million in average annual receipts for most non-manufacturing industries.*

Having an official definition of micro, small and medium-sized enterprises is essential for governments adopting policies and programmes specifically targeted at enterprises by size class.

There is also no universally accepted definition of entrepreneurship, although it is generally linked with enterprise creation. The OECD-Eurostat Entrepreneurship Indicators Programme (EIP, which is explained in the last chapter of this publication) defines entrepreneurs as those persons (business owners) who seek to generate value, through the creation or expansion of economic activity, by identifying and exploiting new products, processes or markets. It is important to note that the EIP concept of entrepreneurship involves innovation and includes failure as important elements of the entrepreneurial process.

* For more detailed definitions see *www.sba.gov/content/what-sbas-definition-small-business-concern.*

Source: OECD, 2011.

Although the detailed analysis of entrepreneurial dynamism through firm creation, expansion and destruction is beyond the scope of this report, the next sub-sections briefly summarise some evidence on its importance throughout the business life cycle.

Start-ups and young firms are often linked to job creation, destruction and economic dynamism

The process of enterprise birth and its role in job creation has been the object of numerous studies – beginning with the work by Birch (1979). At the time, the work claimed to show that two thirds of the increase in employment in the United States between 1969 and 1976 was in firms with fewer than 20 workers. More recently, Stangler and Litan (2009) examined job creation in the United States over 1980-2007 and concluded that job creation primarily occurred in new and young firms. Furthermore, work by Kane (2010) points to start-ups being virtually the sole source of new jobs in the United States.

Less consistent findings have emerged in other studies – and particularly outside the United States. In some instances, this is because of the use of different metrics of job creation. For example, the Kane (2010) study shows that the job creation by start-ups heavily reflects the impossibility of firms' losing jobs in their first year of operation – whereas, once they are two or more years old, they are net shedders of jobs. There are also variations in the contributions of new and small firms depending on macro-economic conditions. Despite concerns over suitable measurement metrics, it is widely accepted that new and small firms can make an important contribution to wealth and job creation in the modern economy.

Evidence points to the distinction between firm size and age. Indeed, although it is often argued that the smallest firms are important (and they certainly are) for employment at a given point of time, what matters the most for job and economic growth is not the size composition of the enterprise population but rather its dynamics. For instance, Haltiwanger et al. (2010) show that, after controlling for firm age, there is no systematic relationship between firm size and job growth. This suggests that the promotion of enterprise creation and the removal of barriers to growth can have an important impact in jobs and economic growth for firms of all sizes and ages.

The youngest and smallest enterprises are also the most likely to disappear in the first years of their existence, therefore leading to important job losses. Stangler and Litan (2009) find that only half of start-ups survive to the fifth year and around a third of them close as soon as their second year of existence. According to Kane (2010), high rates of job creation by start-ups and young firms are accompanied by similar (although normally lower) rates of job losses. This enterprise churn, (the sum of births and deaths of enterprises),[2] is an indicator reflecting the degree of "creative destruction" in an economy and, as argued throughout this report, is of interest for analysing productivity growth (OECD, 2011).

The OECD-Eurostat EIP shows that enterprise births, exits, overall enterprise, and job churn are consistently higher in the services than in the manufacturing sector, reflecting its greater dynamism (OECD, 2011). Furthermore, an analysis of firms in the United Kingdom (Disney et al., 2003) showed that between 1980 and 1992, single establishment firms (25% of manufacturing employment) experienced no productivity growth among survivors; all productivity gains for this group came from entry and exit.

Research by the World Bank, using data from the World Bank Group Entrepreneurship Survey (WBGES), has also revealed that there is a strong and significant relation between firm entry density, total business density and GDP per capita (World Bank, 2008).[3] Similarly, and using WBGES data, Klapper et al. (2008) found that business entry and density rates are significantly related to country-level indicators of economic development and growth, the quality of the legal and regulatory environment, the ease of access to finance, and the prevalence of informality in economic activities. They found that GDP per capita and domestic credit to the private sector (as a percentage of GDP) are both positively and significantly correlated with firm entry rates and business density, suggesting that greater business opportunities and better access to finance are related to a more robust private sector (Klapper et al., 2008).

Along these lines, a study analysing enterprise churn in Jordan, Morocco, Tunisia, and Turkey concludes that enterprise entry and exit in all four economies add to productivity since new firms have higher productivity than survivors and survivors have higher productivity than exiting enterprises. The intensity of churning is significantly lower in Morocco, Tunisia and Jordan than in Turkey (where the churning rates are comparable to east European countries). Thus, low rates of entry are a determinant of low/stagnant rates of productivity growth in MENA. One of the main policy recommendations derived from this study is that more effective competition policies are needed to encourage enterprise entry.

Socio-economic shocks and the quality of business environments have an important impact on the overall entrepreneurial performance of economies

The 2007-09 economic and financial crisis had a negative effect on both enterprise and job creation. A report by the World Bank showed that nearly all countries experienced a sharp drop in business entry rates during the crisis. This drop was particularly sharp in more financially developed countries (Klapper and Love, 2010).

The OECD-Eurostat EIP also found that the crisis had an important effect on the creation of new enterprises: after a significant decrease in the second half of 2008, the number of new enterprises started to recover around the first half of 2009 in most countries. However, by the second quarter of 2010, the number of newly created enterprises was still below its pre-crisis level in most countries (OECD, 2011).

Timely data on enterprise births and exits during the 2011 events is not available for MENA economies. However, the slowdown in economic activity due to political instability and social unrest has almost certainly led to lower rates of enterprise creation (at least of formal firms). Enterprise death rates are likely to have increased, leading to further job losses, adding to those from large company closures and contractions or the departure of foreign investors.

Even before the onset of the first protests at the end of 2010, the MENA region was characterised by stifled enterprise creation. This was the product of a range of factors such as burdensome business environments, low rates of female participation in the economy, bloated public sectors, mismatches between the skills provided by the education systems and the needs of the private sector, high and pervasive levels of corruption and cronyism.

New firms can be important for developing and introducing innovation

Apart from their impact on job creation and economic growth, SMEs and entrepreneurs can also be important sources of technological and non-technological innovation and new and improved products and services. Some authors have argued that, over the last decades, the world economy, mainly in developed countries but also in some emerging economies, has been undergoing a shift from a "managed" to an "entrepreneurial" economy, in which entrepreneurship, start-ups and high growth SMEs play a key role as drivers of competitiveness and growth (Audretsch & Thurik, 2001; Schramm, 2006; and OECD, 2002). For this type of enterprise, intellectual assets are increasingly an important factor of economic value over traditional production factors, while increased competition imposes pressures on both large and small firms which, in order to thrive and even survive, have to innovate constantly.

A 2010 OECD study on SMEs, entrepreneurship and innovation noted that innovation is no longer the exclusive result of investments in research and development and is not limited to the realm of science and technology. Innovation is also the creation of a multitude of new products and services in all sectors of the economy, new marketing methods and changes in the way business organises its practices within the workplace and externally. In this framework, new firm creation through entrepreneurship (which typically generates new SME entities but occasionally also "born large" firms) and innovations in existing SMEs play an important role (OECD, 2010b).

The OECD study also notes that the importance of new and small firms to the innovation process has increased, given relatively recent developments such as increasing incomes, more "niched" markets, and changing technologies, importantly those of the "knowledge economy", which have reduced the structural disadvantage of small firms (OECD, 2010b). This has resulted in the shift from a "managed economy", where competitiveness was mainly based on economies of scale, mass production and standardised products to an "entrepreneurial economy", where SMEs and new ventures play an important role in developing technological and non-technological innovations.[4]

Obviously, this argument does not imply that large firms and investments in R&D and science and technology have decreased their innovative output. Aggregate data shows that large enterprises account for most of the innovative activity; but the roles of small and large firms in the innovation process can be complementary rather than competing. Small and entrepreneurial firms can, for instance, play an important role in introducing and commercialising radical innovations, which are essential for economic and employment growth, while large, well established firms generally refine and mass-produce radical innovations (OECD, 2008).

Innovations from emerging markets

Different factors often drive entrepreneurship and small-firm innovation in developed and developing countries and they are characterised by different traits. Generally, more advanced economies are characterised by business environments relatively conducive to the creation and growth of firms, higher productivity levels and higher levels of education, skills and technology. Developing and emerging economies, in contrast, are often linked to necessity-driven rather than opportunity-driven businesses, by higher levels of economic informality and by lower levels of education and skills.[5]

However, developing and emerging markets are increasingly becoming new sources of business innovation as their income expands, their middle classes grow and new business opportunities and new prospects for entrepreneurs emerge. A palpable example of this is the emergence of "frugal innovations", generally from developing economies, which are products and services based on existing technologies but redesigned to meet the needs and incomes of comparatively poorer sectors of the population (e.g. frugal healthcare devices, water filters, banking business models through mobile telephony, repackaging of products, etc.).

These generalisations do not imply that there are only two "types" of innovations being developed in emerging and developing markets. Nor does it mean that necessity-driven entrepreneurship cannot lead to innovative approaches to business. However, an increasing body of evidence points to the rising role of emerging markets in the development of frugal innovations and in overall innovative activity.

Making the case for high growth enterprises

Job creation, economic dynamism and innovation are clearly linked to entrepreneurial performance, but there are, of course, different "types" of firms in the economy. Following a simplified or stylised view, the small enterprise population can be divided in the following subsets of enterprises:

1. short-life firms that do not survive beyond two years;

2. micro firms that are often necessity-driven, operate in the informal sector and with few growth prospects;

3. a tiny proportion of enterprises that are driven by the pursuit of economic opportunity and that have potential for growth in terms of employment and/or turnover. This type of firm, known as high growth enterprises, is the focus of this report; and

4. particularly in the context of MENA and some other economies, a small share of well-established enterprises (small and large), managed and/or owned by well-connected

business people and which exert a disproportionate market dominance. This type of enterprise, and the competitive pressure that high growth firms can exert on them, will be analysed in the subsequent chapters.

The relevance of short-life and necessity-driven firms should not be denied

Enterprise entry and exit are part of the entrepreneurial performance of economies and are an important element of enterprise and job churn, as new and more productive enterprises create competitive pressures on established enterprises. Many firms exit the market simply because their businesses are of short-term nature (*e.g.* construction projects) or because they operate in declining industries or particular locations. Entrepreneurial success, according to some authors, is also a process involving trial and error from which entrepreneurs learn (Frankish *et al.*, 2012).

Micro, informal (unregistered) and necessity-driven enterprises are essential generators of income and employment, especially for the poorest members of society (Hughes, 2000) and in the absence of social protection systems. According to data from the Global Entrepreneurship Monitor (GEM), emerging economies register higher levels of business creation than high-income countries (see the following chapter). Even so, emerging economies usually have lower levels of productivity and innovation than developed countries.

A small share of firms have exceptionally positive effects on jobs, innovation and productivity

Although there is no single definition for "high growth enterprises", this term usually refers to firms that have exceptionally positive effects on employment, value added and increased productivity. Studies undertaken in OECD countries and some emerging economies have found that these firms represent roughly 4-6% of the enterprise population. These enterprises may be referred to as "high- or fast-growth firms" or "high-impact enterprises", or as "gazelles" when they are young (see Box 1.2). This report uses the term "high growth enterprises", which includes both high growth and gazelles.

Box 1.2. The definition of high growth and high-potential enterprises as used in this report

The OECD and Eurostat (OECD 2011) define high growth SMEs and gazelles as follows:

High growth enterprises, as measured by employment (or by turnover), are firms with average annualised growth in employees (or in turnover) greater than 20% a year, over a three-year period, and with ten or more employees at the beginning of the observation period. The share of high growth enterprises in an economy is calculated as the number of high growth enterprises expressed as a percentage of the population of enterprises with ten or more employees.

Gazelles form a subset of the group of high growth enterprises; they are high growth enterprises born five years or less before the end of the three-year observation period. Measured in terms of employment (or turnover), gazelles are enterprises which have been employers for a period of up to five years, with average annualised growth in employees (or in turnover) greater than 20% a year over a three-year period and with ten or more employees at the beginning of the observation period. The share of gazelles is expressed as a percentage of the population of enterprises with ten or more employees.

All firms analysed in this report are 5 years old or younger, which corresponds to the EIP definition of a gazelle in terms of age.

The report identifies high growth enterprises as the key agents of positive economic change, with a potential to contribute to economic growth directly through employment and value added creation and indirectly by exercising competitive pressure on incumbent firms. Employment (or value added) creation refers to the actual generation of new jobs, as opposed to the expansion of employment in a firm through the merger or acquisition of another company. High growth is not a permanent feature in the life cycle of a company but, much more often, a temporary burst or spurt of growth that can occur one or more times. In other words, high growth is rather a characteristic referring to an event (or several events) in an enterprise and not to an enterprise *per se*, since companies can register one or more periods of fast growth during their existence.

For example, in terms of *economic impact*, Jovanovic (2001) reported that four of the largest companies in the United States, in terms of market capitalisation in August 1999, were under 20 years old. These four companies were Microsoft, Cisco Systems, MCI and Dell. Their total company valuation was equivalent to 13% of the GDP of the United States. This is a huge economic contribution and emphasises the role which rapidly growing small businesses can play over a period, even if the period in question here – the height of the "dot-com" boom – was exceptional; in the years since, the United States has produced other international 'names' to be added to this list.

However, it is not only in the United States where rapidly growing new and small firms have played an important role. Nokia, the Finnish telecommunications company that at the start of the 80s was only a tiny enterprise, grew so rapidly that it, virtually alone, pulled the Finland economy out of recession during the mid-90s (Ali-Yrkkao [eds.], 2010; Powell, 2011). These firms, known alternatively as gazelles or high-impact firms, are of keen interest to scholars and to policy makers.

Along the same lines, Acs *et al.* (2008), analysed "high-impact firms" (rapidly growing firms responding for most employment growth) in the United States and found that from 1994 to 2006 they represented 2-3% of all enterprises, yet accounted for almost all the private sector employment and revenue growth in the economy. Their findings showed that such firms were relatively old, with an average age of 25 years.

This is in line with the OECD finding that high growth is not limited to any particular type of enterprise (*i.e.* those that are young, with an educated managerial staff, in high-tech sectors, active in international markets, etc.) and that a period of high growth is an exceptional event that can occur in the life of virtually any enterprise (OECD, 2010a).

A preliminary overview of high growth enterprises in the MENA region

One of the very few reports on high growth enterprises in the MENA region (Stone and Tarek Badawy, 2011), covering Egypt, Lebanon, Libya, Morocco, Syria and Yemen, identified enterprise characteristics associated with high growth.[6] These were being an innovator, offering workers formal training and receiving an international quality certification. The findings, according to the authors, direct policy attention towards education, training, quality systems, computer literacy and competition policy (broadly understood) as key focal points for a strategy to promote SME-based employment growth (Stone and Tarek Badawy, 2011, p. 1). The results from that survey, however, are based on only one year of growth (except for Egypt, where data was available for three years), thus the direction of causality is unclear. Longitudinal data could help to address these issues, but it is totally lacking in the MENA region.

Chapter 2 of this report uses proxy indicators to identify "high potential" enterprises, or firms that *could* be or become high growth.

Innovation as a driver of high growth

The development or introduction of innovative products or services, new production processes (or delivery of services) and new and better organisational practices is often the result of opportunity seeking and can be an important driver of productivity, competitive pressure on incumbents and ultimately growth.

However, the relationship between innovation and high growth is not straightforward. At the aggregate level, innovation can lead to higher economic growth and employment creation, but at the level of the individual enterprise, innovation can also lead to fewer people being employed in a firm. This is the case in technological innovations that increase productivity by decreasing the quantity of inputs (including labour) needed to produce a unit of output (OECD, 2010a).[7] Furthermore, innovation is not a prerequisite for high growth, which can result from a myriad of factors, such as the rate of economic growth in a country or region, or if the firm operates in a high growth industry. Box 1.3 shows the main conclusion of an OECD study on high growth enterprises (OECD, 2010a).

Box 1.3. Main conclusions from the 2010 OECD study on High Growth Enterprises

The points below summarise the main findings from an OECD study of high growth and innovative SMEs undertaken mainly in OECD countries. Although the findings cannot be translated into concrete policy implications for MENA economies, given the economic and institutional differences (among others) between those economies and OECD countries, they do highlight some revealing elements.

- *High growth is an exceptional event that can occur in the lifetime of almost any enterprise.* It is therefore often a transitory event and not a characteristic of a specific subset of firms. This has important policy implications, in terms of who or what should be the target of policies to promote high firm growth.

- *High growth is attributable to a mix of factors and not a single event.* However, one necessary condition is for the owners to have an ambition to grow.

- *High growth can be disruptive at the managerial, financial and technical resources level.*

- *High growth is correlated to innovation* but the direction of the causation is unclear.

- *There is no generalised credit-rationing problem among innovative and high growth SMEs in the mostly developed countries analysed in the OECD study.* Access to finance issues appear to be country-specific and to depend on the type of source on which the studies are based. In the case of the MENA region, however, access to finance is one of the main issues facing enterprise creation and expansion.

- It is difficult to identify, certainly at start-up, firms that will grow faster based on a list of common characteristics. Therefore, an appropriate policy strategy would be to create the conditions for any firm to become high growth or to experience one or more periods of rapid growth.

Source: OECD, 2010a.

The studies cited above have approached high growth enterprises from different angles and their conclusions are diverse. Some argue that it is start-ups and the youngest firms that have the greatest impact on economic dynamism. Others conclude that high growth is a temporary feature that could happen in any type of firm, regardless of economic sector, size or characteristics of managers at different moments of a firm's existence. All the studies, however, point to the fact that high growth enterprises have a disproportionately positive effect on the economy.

Education and entrepreneurial performance

Several studies in developed and developing countries have found a positive link between education and entrepreneurial performance.[8] For instance, Van der Sluis, van Praag and Vijverberg (2005) aggregated research from more than 80 sources since 1980 and conducted an analysis for developing countries to quantify the effect of general education on entrepreneurial performance. They conclude that a marginal year of schooling for the entrepreneur increases enterprise performance by an average of 5.5 per cent. On average, primary education yields a 19 per cent gain compared to no schooling. Entrepreneurs with secondary schooling earn 34 per cent more and entrepreneurs with postsecondary schooling earn 40 per cent more than unschooled individuals do.

This is slightly lower than the return of education in wage employment (estimates range from 7-11%). Furthermore, the returns of schooling are on average higher for women and for urban residents. They are also higher in agricultural economies, where the general level of education is low.

These results are confirmed by other studies, which have focused on general education, measured in terms of "total years of education", or according to the highest degree obtained such as "secondary school graduate", or "college graduate". Entrepreneurial performance has been measured differently in various studies but included indicators such as "growth in sales", "growth in profits", and "innovation", "growth in personal income", or "income in comparison to wage earners".

This section has shown that, although they are few in numbers, high growth firms can have the potential to make a considerable economic, employment and innovation impact. Such firms are unsurprisingly of interest to policymakers.

The analysis of high-impact firms in the MENA region

High growth firms do not have a consistent and specific set of characteristics and accurately predicting which firms will achieve high growth in the future is very difficult indeed. It is also evident that most studies have focused on OECD countries, and there is scant research on the specific case of the MENA region. Furthermore, the fact that growth is a time-bound feature and the lack of longitudinal data tracking enterprise growth means that it is very difficult to assess the situation of high growth firms, even after fast growth has occurred.

The rationale for this report is that, despite the economic potential of high growth enterprises in the MENA region, there is a paucity of research on their characteristics, the obstacles they face, and the impact of public policy on their ability to grow.

The current levels of socio-political and economic instability, accompanied by high unemployment rates, signal a need to promote growth and particularly homegrown entrepreneurship in order to stimulate economic activity and employment. This is not to say that MENA economies should look exclusively inwards for sources of growth. Instead, given the current low levels of domestic and foreign consumer and investor confidence,

MENA economies should foster domestic talent to supplement job creation in the short term and develop a more entrepreneurial-driven economy in the medium to longer term.

Despite the scarcity of evidence and data, the topic of fast-growing enterprises needs investigation in a MENA context. To circumvent this problem, this report uses firms recently established by graduates as a proxy, because these are likely to have better growth prospects than those established by individuals without this level of formal qualifications – an assumption for which there is some research support in developed countries (van der Sluis *et al.*, 2008).

This report examines the nature and scale of entrepreneurial activity, including high growth enterprises, in the MENA region. It specifically examines in detail a number of high growth enterprises in five MENA countries: Egypt, Jordan, Morocco, Tunisia, and UAE. It aims to provide a comprehensive range of policy options open to policymakers in MENA economies seeking to foster the development and creation of high growth enterprises.

The report addresses three key questions:

- If high growth enterprises are so important for economic growth and employment, are MENA economies generating a significant pool of enterprises with the potential to become high growth and to break the status quo? What are their characteristics vis-à-vis similar enterprises in developed and other emerging economies?

- What obstacles prevent the pool of high potential enterprises from becoming high growth? Is there evidence of an incoming new generation of entrepreneurs with different profiles from incumbents in terms of education, motivations, professional experience and gender?

- Is the business environment conducive to high growth firms? What can public policy do to promote high growth firms and what are MENA governments doing in this regard? What elements are still missing?

Chapter 2 reviews the role of high growth enterprises in the MENA region and provides an overview of entrepreneurship and enterprise creation and development in economies for which data is available.[9] The analysis is based on data from the Global Entrepreneurship Monitoring (GEM) network.

A number of MENA countries have joined the GEM network and have recently conducted adult population surveys to identify those involved in start-up, new and established ventures. This has resulted in the collection of a significant amount of internationally comparable data. The analysis compares the MENA region with other regions and, in addition, focuses on sub-regions within MENA, namely North West Africa (Algeria, Morocco and Tunisia), the Middle East (Egypt, Jordan, Lebanon, Syria and the Palestinian Authority) and the Gulf countries (Saudi Arabia and the United Arab Emirates). Comparisons are made in terms of:

- *enterprise creation and development* during the first five years of the firm;

- the subset of *high-potential firms* using as proxies high-tech enterprises, firms which say they expect to have an impact in the markets in which they operate, firms expecting substantial job growth and firms with export orientations;

- *owner-manager comparisons* by motivation (opportunity- *vs.* necessity-driven entrepreneurs), gender, age groups, educational attainment (years of schooling) and income categories (low, middle and high); and

● *factors associated with business creation*, such as prevalence of informal investors; a composite index reflecting perception of business opportunities, confidence in skills to start a business, and knowing other entrepreneurs; cultural or traditional values; proportion of women participating in work; and levels of population growth over the period 1999-2009.

Chapter 3 moves from the broad picture of enterprise activity to an examination of 20 individual, high growth businesses identified in Egypt, Jordan, Morocco, Tunisia, and the United Arab Emirates. Owners include at least one graduate each and all began trading after 2005. They are by no means restricted to high-tech, or even to "modern", sectors.

Chapter 4 reviews the policy frameworks that governments have in place to promote enterprise and entrepreneurship, and high growth enterprises. These are examined for OECD countries and for the five MENA countries.

Chapter 5 provides conclusions and policy implications. It also points to where there is a need for further research.

Notes

1. The OECD distinguishes the concepts of enterprise birth and enterprise creation. An enterprise creation refers to the emergence of a new production unit. This can be either due to a real birth of the unit, or due to other creation by a merger, break-up, split-off or discontinuity point according to the continuity rules. The concept of enterprise birth is more restrictive than the concept of creation as it refers to a legal entity that appears for the first time with no other enterprise involved in the creation process. It excludes firm creations resulting from mergers or changes of name, type of activity or ownership (OECD, 2011, p. 82).

2. Excluding entries and exits due to mergers, breaks-ups, spin-offs, take-overs, etc.

3. Firm entry density is defined as the number of newly registered corporations divided by the working age population (age 15-65) and normalised by 1 000. Total business density is defined as the number of total registered corporations divided by the working age population and normalised by 1 000.

4. See for instance OECD 2010b, Audretsch and Thurik, 2001, Schramm, 2006 and Baumol, 2002.

5. See, for instance, Autio (2007); Ayyagari *et al.* (2003); and OECD (2004).

6. Based on regional surveys encompassing nearly 3 000 SMEs (employing up to 99 workers) in the manufacturing and services sectors.

7. However, increases in productivity that lead to lower production costs and that are translated in higher demand can increase employment; hence technological innovation can also have a positive effect in job creation.

8. An extensive literature review is provided by Weaver, Mark, Pat Dickson, and Solomon, George. "Entrepreneurship and Education: What is known and not known about the links between education and entrepreneurial activity" The Small Business Economy: A Report to the President (2006): 113-156.

9. A more detailed analysis of this is presented in Reynolds, P. (2013, forthcoming), which is also part of the research leading to this publication.

Bibliography

Acs, Z., W. Parsons and S. Tracy (2008), *High-Impact Firms: Gazelles Revisited*, Corporate Research Board, LLC, Washington, DC.

Ali-Yrkkö, Jyrki (ed.) (2010), *Nokia and Finland in a Sea of Change*, ETLA (ElinkeinoelämänTutkimuslaitos-The Research Institute of the Finnish Economy), Helsinki.

Audretsch, D.B. and A.R.Thurik (2001), "What's New About the New Economy? Sources of Growth in the Managed and Entrepreneurial Economies", *Industrial and Corporate Change*, 10 (1), 267-315.

Autio, E. (2007), *Global Report on High-Growth Entrepreneurship*, Global Entrepreneurship Monitor, London.

Ayyagari, M., T. Beck and A. Demirgüç-Kunt (2003), "Small and Medium Enterprises Across the Globe: A New Database", *World Bank Policy Research Working Paper 3127.*

Baumol, W. (2002), *The Free-Market Innovation Machine: Analyzing the Growth Miracle of Capitalism*, Princeton University Press, Princeton.

Birch, D.L. (1979), *The Job Generation Process*, MIT Press, Cambridge, Massachusetts.

Coad, A., J. Frankish, R.G. Roberts and D.J. Storey (2012), *Growth Paths and Survival Chances: An Application of Gamblers' Ruin Theory*, SPRU-University of Sussex, Brighton.

Disney, R., J. Haskel and Y. Heden (2003), "Restructuring and Productivity Growth in UK Manufacturing", *Economic Journal, 113* (489), 666-694.

Frankish, J., R.G. Roberts, D.J. Storey and A. Coad (2012, forthcoming), "Do Entrepreneurs Really Learn? Or Do They Just Tell Us That They Do?", *Industrial and Corporate Change.*

Haltiwanger, J.C., R.S. Jarmin and J. Miranda (2010), "Who Creates Jobs? Small Vs. Large Vs. Young", *NBER Working Paper Series*, August.

Henrekson, M. and D. Johansson (2010), "Gazelles As Job Creators: A Survey and Interpretation of the Evidence", *Small Business Economics*, 35:227-244.

Hull, L. and R. Arnold (2007), *Size by Turnover of New Zealand Firms and 2000 to 2005: Turnover growth of a cohort of New Zealand firms*, Ministry of Economic Development, Wellington.

Hughes, A. (2000), "On Enlarging Employment by Promoting Small Enterprises", ESRC Centre for Business Research, University of Cambridge, *Working Paper*, No. 180.

Jovanovic, B. (2001), "New Technology and the Small Firm", *Small Business Economics*, 16 (1), 53-55.

Kane, T. (2010), "The Importance of Startups in Job Creation and Job Destruction", *Kauffman Foundation Research Series: Firm Formation and Economic Growth*, July.

Klapper, L., R. Amit and M.F. Guillén, "Entrepreneurship and Firm Formation Across Countries", in J. Lerner and A. Schoar (eds.) (2010), *International Differences in Entrepreneurship* (pp. 129-158), NBER Conference Papers, University of Chicago Press,Chicago.

Klapper, L. and I. Love (2010), "The Impact of the Financial Crisis on New Firm Registration", *World Bank Policy Research Working Paper*, No. 5444.

Nicola, M. (2009), *Middle East – The rising importance of SMEs*, Standard Chartered, Dubai.

OECD (2011), *Entrepreneurship at a Glance 2010*, OECD, Paris.

OECD (2010)a, *High Growth Enterprises: What Governments Can do to Make a Difference*, OECD, Paris.

OECD (2010)b, *SMEs, Entrepreneurship and Innovation*, OECD, Paris.

OECD (2008), *The OECD Kansas City Workshop Message: "High Growth SMEs and Innovation fuel the Entrepreneurial Engine".* Retrieved from OECD: *www.oecd.org/document/8/0,3343,en_2649_201185_40554248_1_1_1_1,00.html.*

OECD (2004), "Promoting SMEs for Development", *Second OECD Conference of Ministers Responsible for SMEs, Promoting Entrepreneurship and Innovative SMEs in a Global Economy*, Istanbul.

OECD (2002), *High Growth SMEs and Employment*, OECD, Paris.

OECD-World Economic Forum (2011), *Arab World Competitiveness Report 2011-2012*, World Economic Forum, Geneva.

Powell, N. (2011), "How Finland Became Hooked on Nokia", *The Globe and Mail*, 26 October.

Reynolds, P. (2013, forthcoming), *Firm Creation in the Business Life Course: MENA Countries in the Global Context*, OECD-IDRC, Paris and Ottawa.

Reynolds, P.D. and R.T. Curtin (eds.) (2011), *New Business Creation.An International Overview*, Springer, New York.

Schramm, C.J. (2006), *Entrepreneurial Capitalism and the End of Bureaucracy: Reforming the Mutual Dialog of Risk Aversion*, American Economic Association, 2006 Meetings, Boston, Massachusetts.

Sekkat, K. (ed.) (2009), *Market Dynamics and Productivity in Developing Countries: Economic Reforms in the Middle East and North Africa*, Springer and IDRC, New York and Ottawa.

Stangler, D., and R.E. Litan (2009), *Where Will the Jobs Come From?*, Ewing Marion Kauffman Foundation, Kansas City, Missouri.

Stevenson, L. (2010), "Understanding Entrepreneurship in MENA: Where to go next", *ICSB Global Entrepreneurship Summit, George Washington University*, Washington, DC.

Stone, A. and L. Tarek Badawy (2011), "SME Innovators and Gazelles in MENA – Educate, Train, Certify, Compete!", World Bank , *MENA Knowledge and Learning, Quick Notes Series*, 43.

Van der Sluis, J., M. van Praag and M. Vijverberg (2008), "Education and Entrepreneurship Selection and Performance: A review of the Empirical Literature", *Journal of Economic Surveys*, 22 (5), 795-841.

Van der Sluis, J., M. van Praag and W. Vijverberg (2005), "Entrepreneurship selection and performance: A meta-analysis of the impact of education in developing economies", *World Bank Economic Review* Vol. 19, No. 2, pp. 225-261.

Weaver, M., P. Dickson, and G. Solomon (2006), "Entrepreneurship and Education: What is known and not known about the links between education and entrepreneurial activity". *The Small Business Economy: A Report to the President (2006)*, Small Business Administration, Washington.

World Bank Development Research Group (DECRG) (2008), "Entrepreneurship and Economic Development: An Overview of the 2008 World Bank Entrepreneurship Survey (WBGES)", *The World Bank Economic Review*, 19(2), 225-261.

ANNEX 1.A1

Facts and statistics on the importance of SMEs and entrepreneurship across countries

This annex presents data and facts on small and medium-sized enterprises and entrepreneurship for some OECD countries and a few emerging and MENA economies. The data show a general, although inevitably incomplete, picture. The statistics are not comparable across countries, with the exception of OECD data. This lack of data comparability/availability and the significant economic and institutional differences between OECD and MENA countries have to be considered when drawing policy implications for SME development in general and gazelles in particular. The data and information presented below, however, highlight general evidence on the weight of SMEs and high-impact enterprises in developed, developing and emerging economies.

Some key indicators of the importance of SMEs

- According to the OECD (2011), 97% to 99% of the entire **enterprise population** in countries for which data are available are SMEs; microenterprises are the predominant type of firms in many cases.

- Data from the **MENA region** is scarce, but evidence suggests that SMEs comprise 95% of private enterprises (totalling some 12 million SMEs) and that the majority of those SMEs have fewer than five workers (Stevenson, 2010). According to Standard Chartered (2009), micro firms represent 89% of all firms in Jordan, 93% in Egypt and 97% in Lebanon.

- The weight of SMEs in **employment** varies, ranging from 43% of total employment in the Slovak Republic to over 80% in Italy (OECD, 2011), and 74% in Egypt and over 80% in the UAE and Saudi Arabia (Standard Chartered, 2009).

- The contribution of SMEs to **value-added** is lower, although still significant: three quarters of total value added in Greece, compared to less than a third in Ireland (OECD, 2011), and in the MENA region estimates range from 30% in the UAE to 80% in Egypt (Standard Chartered, 2009).

- Although the contribution by SMEs to **exports** is generally lower than that of larger firms, it is far from negligible: ranging from less than a quarter of total exports in the United States to over 50% in Italy (OECD, 2011). No estimates are available for MENA countries.

Evidence points to the significance of entrepreneurship and enterprise dynamics

- A 2011 study suggests that roughly one in every ten individuals in the world is involved in business creation (Reynolds and Curtin, 2011).

- OECD analysis of a group of developed and emerging economies indicates that the services sector shows more dynamism than the manufacturing sector in terms of enterprise creation, enterprise survival after one year of birth, and employment. In other words, there are more firms and employment *created and destroyed* in the services than in the manufacturing sector, and manufacturing firms have a higher survival rate than services ones (OECD, 2011).

- Data from New Zealand suggests that over a five-year period 8% of firms increase their sales, 40% remain stable, 30% cease trading and 22% shrink (Hull and Arnold, 2008).

- In the case of the United Kingdom, evidence indicates that 60% of new businesses cease within five years (Frankish *et al.*, 2011) and that the median new firm, even if it survives, increases its sales for only three years – after that its sales fall (Coad *et al.*, 2011).

The impact of high growth enterprises and gazelles

- In developed countries, the bulk of economic impact amongst new and small firms is concentrated in a tiny minority – perhaps 4% of new firms create 50% of the jobs in a decade (Henrekson and Johansson, 2010).

- Evidence from the OECD-Eurostat Entrepreneurship Indicators Programme (EIP) on high growth enterprises also shows that those firms represent on average a small share of firm population, typically between 3.5% and 6% when measured by employment growth (see Box 1.2 for a definition of high growth enterprises and gazelles). However, when growth is measured by turnover, the share of high growth enterprises is higher, with percentages going to over 20% (OECD, 2011).

- Data from some OECD and emerging economies shows that high growth firms are more frequent in the services sector if they are measured by employment; however, when the measure is turnover, their prevalence is higher in the manufacturing sector (OECD, 2011). This may reflect the fact that services tend to be more labour-intensive compared to manufacturing, which is more capital-intensive.

- In terms of gazelles (*i.e.* high growth firms younger than five years), data from the EIP shows that these are even fewer, accounting for less than 1% (and even less than 0.5% in some cases) of the enterprise population if they are measured in terms of employment. When measured in terms of turnover, their share is slightly higher. Interestingly, in some European ex-transition economies, gazelles represent a share up to 4%, depending on the growth criteria (OECD, 2011).

Chapter 2

Enterprise development and entrepreneurship in the MENA region

Based on data for several economies, this chapter analyses the levels and characteristics of entrepreneurship and enterprise development in MENA in a global context and across sub-regions of MENA. The chapter presents an overview of the prevalence of firms in different stages of the business life course and the distribution across economic sectors. Then it focuses on the prevalence of "high-potential" firms or firms that could be or become high growth. The third section of the chapter focuses on the nature of the individuals involved as owner-managers and differing motivations that can influence enterprise success.

The analysis in this chapter is mostly based on data from the Global Entrepreneurship Monitor (GEM). A more extensive statistical analysis is published in P. Reynolds, (2013, forthcoming), Firm Creation in the Business Life Course: MENA Countries in the Global Context, OECD and IDRC, Paris and Ottawa, which is also part of the research leading to this publication.

Introduction

Although high growth enterprises represent a tiny share of all firms, the phenomenon of high growth is not exclusive to a specific subset of firms and is therefore not limited to small firms, innovative companies, those managed by highly educated staff or any other specific type of enterprise. Indeed, high growth can occur in an enterprise, of any size and age, operating in any sector of economic activity, in any country and can be driven by a myriad of factors, internal or/and external to the firm, including high economic growth, a booming exporting industry, high growth of customer companies, the introduction of innovations and so on.

This chapter analyses four main areas of interest for entrepreneurship and enterprise development in the MENA region, including for high growth firms:

1. a description of the ratio of firms in different stages of the business life course and in different economic sectors per 100 adults aged 18-64 (defined as *enterprise prevalence*);

2. a description of the *enterprise prevalence* of four types of firms with potential to be or to become high growth: those employing staff with technical skills; those expecting to have a major impact on local markets; those anticipating growth in employment; and firms oriented towards international markets and tourism. These firms are named "high potential" enterprises;

3. an analysis of the nature of individuals involved as owner-managers; and

4. an assessment of factors associated with business creation in higher- and lower-income MENA economies.

The analysis draws extensively from data from the Global Entrepreneurship Monitor (GEM) and uses international comparisons. The use of aggregate GEM data to analyse MENA economies as a group represents a new contribution to research on entrepreneurship in the region. Previous studies have used GEM data to analyse individual MENA economies, but to date no study had pooled data to identify regional characteristics and performance.

Concepts and terminology

The main source of information in this chapter is the Global Entrepreneurship Monitor programme, which provides estimates of the prevalence rates of firms in different stages in the business life course. Box 2.1 below provides a short description of the GEM.

The stages in the life course of a firm

What matters for employment creation and economic dynamism is not the structure or composition of the population of firms itself but the dynamics of new enterprise creation and exit, whereby incumbents have to keep competitive or risk being pushed out of business by new, more competitive and innovative ventures (a creative destruction process). As such, entrepreneurial activity is a dynamic process that displays different characteristics at different stages (Box 2.1 above provides a definition of entrepreneurial

Box 2.1. **About the Global Entrepreneurship Monitor**

The Global Entrepreneurship Monitor (GEM) programme was established to provide harmonised measures of participation in the firm life course that were independent of existing national registries, which all use different criteria for identifying active firms and adding new listings. This information can be used to explore factors affecting national variations in business creation and its role in national economic growth.

The GEM programme is a collaborative effort among self-funded national teams. Interviews with representative samples of adults 18-64 years of age are the basis for identifying those active as nascent entrepreneurs or as active owner managers of profitable firms. The overview in Chapter 2 is based on data available at the time of preparation, which involved surveys completed from 2000 to 2009 in 75 countries and involving 1.1 million screening interviews. (Additional countries and screening interviews are added each year.) In most cases, each country is represented by a minimum of 2 000 screening interviews. However, the sample size is often not large enough, especially where national entrepreneurial activity rates are low, to permit detailed analysis of the characteristics of the business involved. Case weights are assigned in each country for each year such that the GEM samples match the best national data on basic demographics.

All respondents complete a short list of initial items related to participation in the firm life course, attitudes toward business creation, and basic socio-demographic characteristics. Those identified as active in the firm life course list additional items about the nature of the business venture and their involvement. Those that report they have been active in creating a new firm, expect to own some or all of the firm, and have not yet realised profits to pay wages or salaries for more than three months are considered nascent entrepreneurs. Those active owner-managers of ventures with profits for more than three months are considered firm owners. The assessments in this chapter are based on about 40 000 nascent entrepreneurs and 90 000 firm managers.

The number of prospective or actual owners, which averages about 1.8 per firm, is used to estimate the number of ventures involved; additional information on the economic sector, current and prospective employment, export activity, and impact on markets served characterise the impact of the ventures. Additional items asked of all screening respondents is used to determine the capacity for entrepreneurship, whether realised or not by involvement in business creation, as well as the extent to which the national context is supporting of entrepreneurship.

The unique advantages of the GEM dataset are the focus on the behaviour associated with firm creation, rather than questions about aspirations for entrepreneurship, and harmonisation of procedures across all countries. In addition, the scope of activities covers all active business activity registered and unregistered; official registers do not capture many ventures in the informal sectors and may be slow to delist inactive cases. On the other hand, there is no independent verification of the accuracy of the reports of GEM respondents.

GEM data are analysed and published in country reports and in an aggregate global report published annually. Analysis of GEM data pooled regionally (and sub-regionally) as here for MENA economies has never been done before.

Detailed information about the GEM project and selected datasets are available on the project website "*www.gemconsortium.org*". Reynolds *et al.* (2005) provides a review of the data collection methodology.

Source: Reynolds et al. (2005).

activity in the context of the GEM). Based on this, the following sections analyse four specific stages in the life course of a business. These are:

1. Nascent business, which are start-up ventures with profits for less than three months.

2. Infant business, which are operating firms with profits for four months or 2.5 years.

3. Young business, which are operating firms with profits for over 2.5 years and up to 5.5 years.

4. Mature business, which are operating firms with profits for over 5.5 years.

It is important to note that the GEM data focuses on firms generating a profit and not on enterprises in general, which are likely to register losses, mostly at the beginning of their operations. The rationale for this approach is that obtaining a profit is one of the ultimate goals of an enterprise and represents a watershed in the lifecycle of a company. By considering firms already registering a profit, the GEM focuses on firms that already have some level of success.

Geographical coverage

The 75 GEM countries compared in this section are shown in Table 2.1 and represent over 90% of the world population. Two broad categories are used: developed and emerging economies.

The rationale for this simplified classification is to bring to light wider commonalities and trends, even though it is understood that some countries classified as developed (Bosnia and Herzegovina, Kazakhstan, FYROM, etc.) or emerging (Angola, Bolivia, Jamaica, etc.) do not fully correspond to those categories. Furthermore, some of the broad characteristics of the private sector are generally similar among emerging economies (i.e. higher levels of necessity rather than opportunity driven entrepreneurship, higher shares of informal economy, greater shares of micro-enterprises, etc.). Therefore, despite some limitations, the classification does provide useful insights.

Six country groups are also analysed. Three of those country groups are often used in international comparisons: **Europe** (which also includes Israel, Kazakhstan and Turkey), **Latin American and the Caribbean**, and **MENA**. The other three are atypical due to data availability (only three countries in **Africa, Sub-Sahara**), levels of development (**higher and lower income Asia**) and cultural proximity but geographical distance (**North America, Oceania**).

Entrepreneurial activity in the MENA region is compared with these six groups of countries and with the two broad categories of developed and developing economies.

The data for all countries was consolidated across all available years, giving equal weight to each year. For some countries (e.g. Morocco) data is available for only one year whereas for others (e.g. the United States) data is available for 10 years (2000-2009).

A sub-regional analysis of the MENA region is also undertaken based on three economy sub-groups:

● North West Africa: Algeria, Morocco, and Tunisia;

● the Middle East: Egypt, Jordan, Lebanon, Syria and the Palestinian Authority; and

● Gulf countries: Saudi Arabia and the United Arab Emirates.

The North West Africa and Middle East regions include economies that are labour-abundant and with no or small availability of hydrocarbons, with the exclusion of Algeria and to a lesser extent Egypt. These countries have low to medium per capita income levels.

Table 2.1. **Global groups in the Global Entrepreneurship Monitor**

	Group name	Countries
Developed	Higher Income Asian	Hong Kong, Japan, South Korea, Singapore, and Taiwan.
	Europe[1]	Austria, Belgium, Bosnia and Herzegovina, Croatia, Czech Republic, Denmark, Finland, France, Germany, Greece, Hungary, Iceland, Israel, Ireland, Italy, Kazakhstan, Latvia, the Former Yugoslav Republic of Macedonia, Netherlands, Norway, Poland, Portugal, Romania, Russia, Serbia, Slovenia, Spain, Sweden, Switzerland, Turkey, and the United Kingdom.
	North America, Oceania	Australia, Canada, New Zealand and the United States.
Emerging	Middle East and North Africa[2]	Algeria, Egypt, Jordan, Lebanon, Morocco, Syria, Tunisia, Palestinian Authority, Saudi Arabia and the United Arab Emirates.
	Lower Income Asian	China, India, Indonesia, Iran, Malaysia, Philippines and Thailand.
	Latin America and the Caribbean	Argentina, Bolivia, Brazil, Chile, Colombia, Dominican Republic, Ecuador, Jamaica, Mexico, Peru, Uruguay and Venezuela.
	Africa, Sub-Sahara	Angola, South Africa and Uganda.

1. Because there is little difference in the level of business creation activity, nine eastern and central European low-income countries are included in the European group: Bosnia & Herzegovina, Croatia, Kazakhstan, Latvia, Macedonia, Poland, Romania, Russia, and Serbia. Most are slightly below the threshold for high income countries of an annual per capita income of USD 20 000.
2. Two high-income countries, Saudi Arabia and United Arab Emirates, are included in the MENA group.
Source: Reynolds, P. (2013, forthcoming), p. 5.

The Gulf countries are rich in hydrocarbon resources, with relatively small populations, and register high levels of income per capita.

Enterprise prevalence in different stages of the business life course

The initial focus of this section concerns the size of the population of *active* enterprises in the MENA region, that is to say, enterprises currently in operation and not only registered firms.

Although there is no optimal figure to use as benchmark, some insights can be drawn by comparing the MENA region with the other country groups. Significant differences in prevalence rates, or the ratio of active enterprise to the total adult population (aged 18-64), may provide insights of differences in the dynamics of entrepreneurial activity (start-up and survival).

The high levels of enterprise prevalence in emerging economies are driven by informal, necessity-driven and micro-enterprises

This sub-section estimates enterprise population in the different stages of the business life course (nascent, infant, young and mature) based on the concept of *enterprise or firm prevalence*, which is defined as the ratio of firms in each stage per 100 adults aged 18-64 years. This concept provides a relative measure that allows comparisons of firms in each stage of the business life course for countries or groups of countries with different population sizes.

The analysis of the GEM data shows that the enterprise prevalence rates are higher in emerging economies than in developed ones. This suggests a negative correlation between enterprise population and income per capita. In other terms, there are proportionally more active enterprises in lower income countries than in higher income ones.

The number of firms is swollen by sole or micro-entrepreneurs who have entered into a business activity by necessity, rather than by opportunity. As noted in the *GEM 2009 Global Report*, in countries with low levels of income per capita, the national economy is characterised by the prevalence of very small businesses (Bosma and Levie, 2010).

In both emerging, as well as in some developed economies, micro-enterprises account for an important share of active enterprise population. However, micro-enterprises in emerging economies tend have lower levels of productivity. Therefore, the presence of a very large number of enterprises, indicated by a high prevalence rate, is not necessarily a positive indicator of economic development and high growth entrepreneurship. What matters more than the number of active enterprises is how many of them are growing and generating increasing amounts of value added and jobs.

The creation and development of formal and informal firms in MENA is lower than in emerging economies

The data in Figure 2.1 shows that enterprise creation and development levels in MENA are lower than most other emerging economies and generally higher than most developed economies. Among lower income countries, only sub-Saharan Africa has a lower prevalence rate of mature enterprises than MENA.

Figure 2.1. Enterprise prevalence in MENA is generally lower than in other emerging economies and is skewed towards nascent and mature firms

Prevalence of enterprises by stage in the business life course

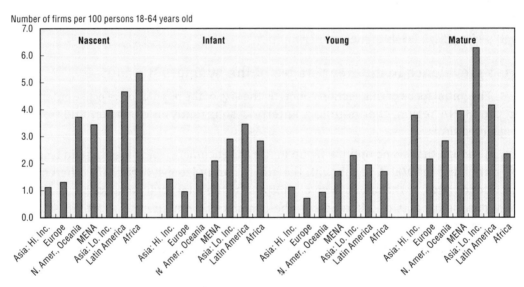

Notes:
Nascent: Profits for less than three months.
Infant: Profits for four months or 2.5 years.
Young: Profits for over 2.5 years and up to 5.5 years.
Mature: Profits for over 5.5 years.
Source: Reynolds (2013, forthcoming).

A closer look at Figure 2.1 also shows that within the MENA region, firms in the nascent and mature stages represent higher shares than those in the intermediate stages of the business life course and therefore, enterprise age is skewed towards both the youngest and the oldest firms.[1] This implies that there are high rates of enterprise mortality between fourth months and 5.5 years of the life of the business, and smaller mortality rates afterwards.

Therefore, it is possible to assume that the prevalence rate in the infant stage largely determines the prevalence rate at the later stages and that the MENA region starts from a weaker position than other emerging economies in terms of firm survival at the very early stage (three months). In other words, fewer firms being created and developed are translated into a smaller firm population from which high growth enterprises (and all enterprises in general) are drawn.

MENA economies differ at the sub-regional level, with significantly higher prevalence rates in North West Africa than in the Gulf countries (Figure 2.2). Furthermore, the entrepreneurial activity in all stages of the business life course in North West African economies is comparable to that of other emerging economies. However, entrepreneurial activity in the Middle East is noticeably lower when compared with the North West Africa region and other emerging economies.

Figure 2.2. **Enterprise prevalence in North West Africa is similar to that of other emerging economies**

Prevalence of enterprises by stage in the business life course

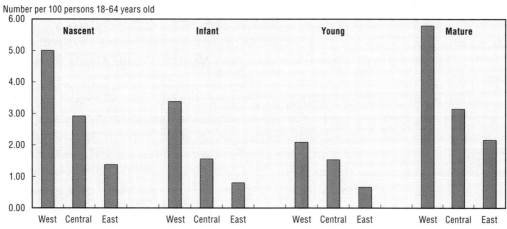

Notes:
Nascent: Profits for less than three months.
Infant: Profits for four months or 2.5 years.
Young: Profits for over 2.5 years and up to 5.5 years.
Mature: Profits for over 5.5 years.
Source: Reynolds (2013, forthcoming).

The gap in the Gulf is wider in the infant and nascent stages, where entrepreneurial activity rates are close to half of what is registered in North West Africa. Furthermore, the prevalence rates in the Gulf countries are well below those of other high-income countries. The gap is particularly wide for mature enterprises, which may be a hint that successful business activities are the domain of a limited number of well-established and well-connected entrepreneurs.

Enterprise creation is even lower if only formally registered firms are considered

Evidence and studies from other sources also point to the low levels of enterprise creation and development in MENA economies. A report by the International Development Research Centre (IDRC) focusing on seven MENA economies and using GEM data also found that developing MENA economies register low levels of early stage entrepreneurial activity rates for countries at their level of development and that most have fewer early stage entrepreneurs than might be expected (IDRC, 2010).

Data from the World Bank Group Entrepreneurship Survey (WBGES) also shows that there is a wide variation in firm-entry density across regions and country income groups. Higher income countries registered, on average, four new firms per 1 000 working-age people (15-65 years) in the period 2004-2009. MENA countries, on the other hand, registered only 0.63 new firms (ahead of only sub-Saharan Africa). Furthermore, the entrepreneurial performance of individual MENA economies for which data are available is lower than that of large developed and emerging economies (World Bank, 2011).

However, there is a significant difference between the GEM and the WBGES data. The former comprises both the formal and the informal sectors, whereas WBGES data are based on newly registered *limited liability firms* as a share of the working-age population in a country. This is why higher income countries lead over emerging and developing economies in terms of firm-entry density.

Along these lines, a Global Entrepreneurship and Development Index (Acs and Autio, 2010), which ranks 71 countries in terms of their performance in the creation of high growth enterprises and high-performance entrepreneurship,[2] revealed that MENA economies lag behind most developed and emerging economies. Eight MENA economies were included in the ranking, with the UAE being the best MENA performer (24th), followed by Saudi Arabia (30th); Egypt (50th); Jordan (51st); Tunisia (58th); Morocco (59th); Algeria (61st); and Syria (68th).

All this evidence substantiates the poor performance of the private sector in the MENA region. However, there is a need for further evidence and analysis to determine if these results are linked to levels of economic development or to other specific factors and, if so, it may well be that those factors also have an influence on the survival and development of high-potential enterprises. Hence, further research tracking specific firms over their life cycle (at least over their initial stages) would greatly enrich the policy debate, not only for the promotion of enterprise creation, but also for the development of high growth enterprises.

Sectors of economic activity in the different stages of the business life course

The proportion of firms in different economic sectors across the stages of the business life course gives some insight about the activity of those enterprises and their contribution to value added. The analysis focuses on four broad economic sectors:

- **Extractive activities** comprise agriculture, forestry, fishing, timber harvesting, and mining (including oil production).
- **Transformative activities** are those that change the form or location of physical items, such as construction, manufacturing, transportation, and wholesale.
- **Business services** are activities in which the primary consumer is a business entity, including finance, insurance, real estate and consulting of all types.
- **Customer-oriented** activities primarily serve people and include all retail, lodging, restaurants and bars, personal services, repair shops, entertainment, leisure, recreation, health, social and educational services.

MENA economies register lower shares of firms in business services activities and higher shares in customer-oriented activities

What emerges from a first glance at the distribution of firms by economic sectors is that MENA economies are similar to other emerging economies: most enterprises are customer-oriented and a lower share is in the business services sector (Figure 2.3). In particular, MENA firms in business services represent on average 10% of firms for all life cycle stages. While this is comparable to the shares in other emerging economies, it is generally less than half the proportion found in the high-income countries.

At the sub-regional level, the Middle Eastern economies are characterised by relatively higher shares of customer-oriented firms than the North West African and Gulf economies, at all stages of the business life course. This in turn is associated with a lower proportion of business service and transformative sector firms in the Middle East, compared to the North West Africa and the Gulf sub-regions. The high proportion of customer-oriented firms in the central region may reflect either a high focus on this sector, a reduced focus on transformative and business services, or a combination of both factors.

Figure 2.3. **Firms in business services activities appear to be under-represented in MENA compared to high-income countries**

Share of firms by economic sector and stage of business life course

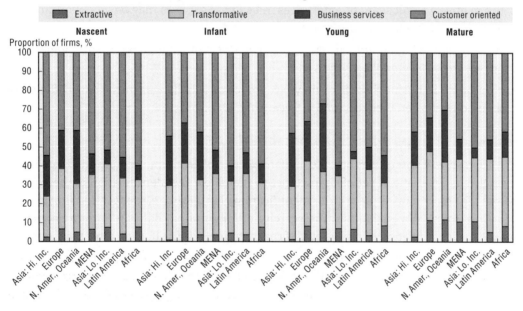

Notes:
Nascent: Profits for less than three months.
Infant: Profits for four months or 2.5 years.
Young: Profits for over 2.5 years and up to 5.5 years.
Mature: Profits for over 5.5 years.
Source: Reynolds (2013, forthcoming).

Fostering the development of business services could prove key for increasing employment and for creating entrepreneurial opportunities for highly educated people

While high growth firm creation can occur in any economic sector, the business services sector may be more likely to foster this type of firm creation. The MENA-OECD

Investment Programme has voiced the need for the MENA region to foster the development of the services sector in general and the business services sector in particular (OECD-World Economic Forum, 2011).

Business services comprise many dynamic economic activities that can contribute to economic diversification, given the variety of services and their high value added. They have a greater tradability potential than traditional services, which could be important for increasing the regional and global economic integration of MENA economies. Business services also foster the adoption and development of innovations and promote economic dynamism and productivity by creating labour demand and entrepreneurial opportunities for highly skilled and educated people (OECD-World Economic Forum, 2011).

When looking at the sectorial performance by stages of the business life course, the GEM data shows that business services firms in MENA economies represent around 11% of all firms in the nascent and infant stages, which are higher shares than those of other emerging economies (although only slightly higher than in Latin America). However, their share significantly falls to 5.5% in the young stage to rise again to 10.5% for mature firms. This implies that enterprises in the business sector face important survival challenges between the age of 2.5 and 5.5 years.

The analysis of the data therefore shows that:

1. the relatively small share of enterprises in business services may be an opportunity for growth for high potential enterprises;

2. there might be high entry barriers and/or low levels of willingness of entrepreneurs to engage in that sector of activity; and

3. enterprises in business services may face important challenges in the consolidation of their activity when they reach 2.5-5.5 years old.

The prevalence of firms with "high potential"

High growth enterprises operate in many sectors of economic activity and there is not a single characteristic or set of characteristics that allow the identification of these firms before high growth takes place (prior identification). Furthermore, the fact that firm growth is a time-bound dimension and the scarcity of longitudinal data on enterprise growth makes the identification of high growth firms extremely difficult, even after the fact.[3]

To overcome these limitations, at least partially, and to provide some insights for international comparison, the focus can be placed on "**high-potential**" enterprises, that is to say, enterprises that could show some of the features of high growth firms such as high growth in employment or turnover.

Four indicators included in the GEM surveys are used as proxy for high potential.

1. the share of firms in sectors likely to employ staff with comparatively high technical skills (*i.e.* employees with scientific, engineering or technological training);

2. the share of firms that expect to have an impact on the markets in which they operate;

3. the share of firms expecting job growth; and

4. the proportion of firms with an emphasis in tourism and foreign markets.

These indicators and the main insights drawn from their analysis are presented in the subsections below. Given the scarcity of data for African countries, the country group "Africa" is excluded from the analysis of high-potential enterprises.

Firms employing staff with technical skills represent, on average, higher shares than in other emerging economies, especially at the mature stage

The first indicator for analysing high-potential firms is the share of **firms in sectors likely to employ staff with comparatively high technical skills** (*i.e.* employees with scientific, engineering, or technological training backgrounds), based on an assessment of the North American Industry Classification System (NAICS).[4] Although these firms are characterised as high-technology enterprises in studies using GEM data, for the purposes of this report it makes more sense to describe them only as employing technical staff, given the great difficulty to characterise certain firms as high-tech based only on this indicator.

To cite a few examples, the highest level in this category includes computer; navigational equipment; data processing and scientific R&D firms. The second highest level includes oil and gas extraction; basic chemical manufacturing; audio and video equipment manufacturing, management; and scientific and technical consulting services. The third level includes paint, coating and adhesive manufacturing; electrical equipment manufacturing; securities and commodity exchanges; electronic and precision equipment repair and maintenance; etc. The analysis in this report uses all three levels.

The rationale for choosing this proxy for high potential is that firms with high technical skills often develop or introduce innovations that would lead to higher than average productivity and competitiveness levels. This can give those firms a competitive advantage over other incumbent firms or can even lead to the creation of markets by introducing a new product or service. However, it is important to note that this is not to say that firms identified by the proxy described above, will necessarily introduce technological innovations.

GEM data shows that this type of high-potential firm represents a higher average in MENA than in other emerging economies over the four stages of the business life course (nearly 12% compared to less than 10% in other emerging economies). Furthermore, their share is relatively steady during the first two stages of the business life cycle. In contrast, all groups of economies and especially Asian countries (including emerging ones) register significant decreases from nascent to infant firms (Figure 2.4). This may indicate that these firms have greater rates of survival during the first 2.5 years of their lives in the case of the MENA region.

Their share in MENA, however, falls to 7.5% at the young stage, to rise again to 15% at the mature stage, which suggests that this type of firm may face hurdles to survival between the 2.5 and the 5.5 years of existence. Furthermore, Figure 2.4 shows that mature firms employing staff with technical skills represent a higher share in MENA than in all other groups of countries.

Some MENA economies have relatively high shares of university graduates in the overall population. This may suggest that the overall higher shares of firms employing staff with technical skills may not be unexpected, especially in the Middle East sub-region. However, the greater survival rates of these firms during the first 2.5 years seem an interesting trend that would deserve further analysis.

The sub-regional analysis of GEM data indicates that North West African economies have lower shares of high-potential firms employing staff with technical skills than the other two MENA sub-regions.

Figure 2.4. **Firms employing staff with high technical skills may face hurdles to their survival between the infant and young stages, but mature firms represent a higher proportion than in other country groups**

Share of firms with high technical skills and by stage of business life course

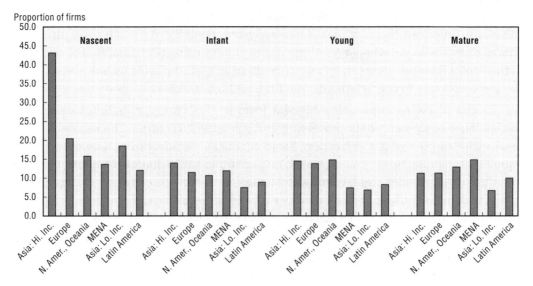

Notes:
Nascent: Profits for less than three months.
Infant: Profits for four months or 2.5 years.
Young: Profits for over 2.5 years and up to 5.5 years.
Mature: Profits for over 5.5 years.

Source: Reynolds (2013, forthcoming).

Firms expecting to have an impact on the markets in which they operate are significantly higher in MENA than in any other group of economies

Firms expecting to have an **impact on the markets** in which they compete are those that, when surveyed by the GEM, responded that they had no competitors, had customers unfamiliar with the product or service, and that they used new technologies. This proxy could represent a mixture of technological and non-technological innovation (*i.e.* firms whose customers are unfamiliar with the products/services they offer or that have no competitors might be introducing a product/service innovation or a new to the market innovation). However, impact on the market may or may not be associated with growth expectations.

The interpretation of this index can vary depending on the context. To cite two extreme examples, a firm creating a new software product for sale to the global market may have a different response to the items than a new firm providing mobile telephony for the first time in a remote area. Both firms may report they expect to have a major market impact; however, the innovativeness of their product may vary dramatically in an absolute sense.

Figure 2.5 shows that the shares of market-impact firms in MENA are significantly higher than in all other regions at all stages of the business life cycle. The shares of market-impact firms in emerging Asia are also higher than in other regions, but not as high as in MENA. This may reflect the rapid transformation of customer-oriented sectors of MENA economies, with the introduction of retail and service businesses familiar to customers in developed countries to new customers in MENA.

Figure 2.5. **The proportion of firms expecting to have an impact in their markets is significantly higher than in all other regions at all stages of the business life course**

Share of firms expecting impact in their markets and by stage of business life course

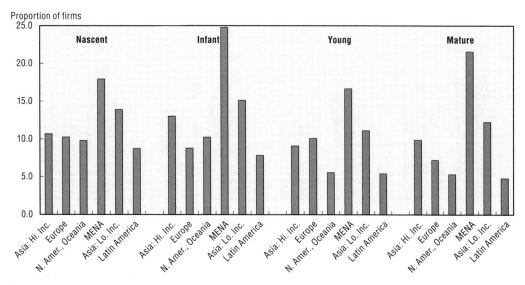

Notes:
Nascent: Profits for less than three months.
Infant: Profits for four months or 2.5 years.
Young: Profits for over 2.5 years and up to 5.5 years.
Mature: Profits for over 5.5 years.
Source: Reynolds (2013, forthcoming).

Market-impact firms also register high shares within all three MENA sub-regions, especially in the Gulf sub-region, where they average a quarter of all firms in the first two stages of the business life course and over 30% during the young and mature stages. The proportion of firms expecting to have an impact in the markets is lowest for the Middle Eastern region among nascent, young and mature firms; there is no regional intraregional difference for infant firms.

The share of firms expecting job growth in MENA is relatively steady over the business life course

The assessment in GEM interviews of **growth in employment** is conducted by asking about the number of jobs to be provided in five years. This is perhaps the most straightforward indicator of high potential, since the most important quality looked at in high growth firms is employment creation.

Those firms expecting 20 or more jobs are considered, relatively speaking, to have growth prospects. Certainly, choosing 20 jobs as a cut-off for high growth may seem subjective and it may seem easier for the largest firms to achieve this or a higher number of new employees. However, it is necessary to consider that the vast majority of enterprises in any country are small, and even more in the case of the youngest firms, which often have no employees other than the owner/manager.

Figure 2.6 shows that firms expecting employment growth represent, on average, greater shares in developed than in emerging economies. In the case of the MENA region, the average share of job growth-oriented firms is lower than that of developed countries

Figure 2.6. **The share of firms which expect growth in employment are similar in MENA to other emerging economy groups**

Share of firms expecting growth in employment and by stage of business life course, 2009

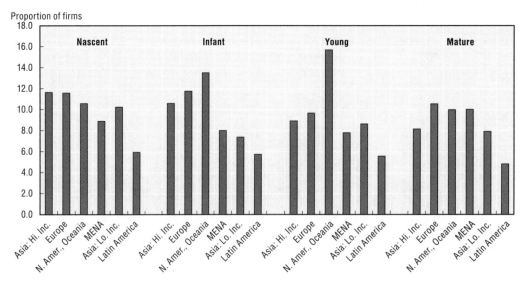

Notes:
Nascent: Profits for less than three months.
Infant: Profits for four months or 2.5 years.
Young: Profits for over 2.5 years and up to 5.5 years.
Mature: Profits for over 5.5 years.

Source: Reynolds (2013, forthcoming).

(8.7 in MENA against 9.8 in high-income Asia, 10.9 in Europe and 12.4 in North America). On the other hand, their share in MENA is similar to that in low-income Asia (8.5) and higher than that of Latin America (5.5). This suggests that the MENA region does not appear to have any specific disadvantage in job creation, compared to other emerging economies.

The share of firms in MENA expecting to create jobs remains relatively steady at around 8% during the first three stages of the business life course. However, they represent 10% of all firms at the mature stage, which is a comparatively higher share than other emerging economies and similar to that of the developed economies in Europe and North America-Oceania. Hence, mature firms have greater job potential than younger ones, although not by a large margin (10% of mature firms versus 9% of nascent ones).

The sub-regional analysis shows that the Gulf economies register significantly higher shares of firms expecting job growth than the other two sub-regions in MENA: over 25% of all firms during the first stages of the business life course and around 20% during the other two stages (Figure 2.7). This is significantly higher than in other MENA economies and higher than in developed and emerging economies (Figure 2.6). The Gulf countries, thus, push the share of firms expecting job growth in the MENA region upwards to a significant degree.

The share of firms oriented towards tourism and foreign markets is larger in MENA than in all other groups of economies at all stages of the business life course

Firms **oriented towards tourism and foreign markets** are those with 25% or more of their total customers residing outside the country.[5] Although this threshold seems subjective, it can provide an approximate measure of potentially high growth enterprises

Figure 2.7. **The share of firms expecting job growth is significantly higher in Gulf countries than in other MENA economies**

High job growth firms: MENA regions by firm life course stage

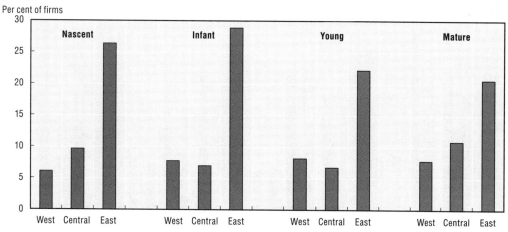

Notes:
Nascent: Profits for less than three months.
Infant: Profits for four months or 2.5 years.
Young: Profits for over 2.5 years and up to 5.5 years.
Mature: Profits for over 5.5 years.

Source: Reynolds (2013, forthcoming).

since they can rely on markets larger than the domestic one. This is more relevant for countries with small domestic markets. Furthermore, the majority of firms serve domestic and even local markets and only a few venture to foreign markets, which could indicate some level of ambition from their owners-managers (although this is not necessarily the case of firms oriented towards tourism).

The share of firms oriented towards tourism and foreign markets in MENA economies is significantly higher than in other emerging economies at all stages of the business life course (Figure 2.8). This is similar to the case of firms with market impact.

This might reflect the large domestic markets in some emerging economies outside MENA (*e.g.* Brazil, China, India and Mexico) and the relatively large tourism sector in some MENA economies (Egypt, Jordan, Lebanon, Morocco, etc.). Furthermore, the share is much higher than in all groups of economies in the mature stage, which means that firms oriented towards tourism and exports are rather well established.

Again, when analysing the percentages of firms across different stages in the business life course, it is possible to see that although the trends are similar to those of enterprise prevalence in general, with more firms in the nascent and mature stages (Figure 2.1), their overall shares remain stable over the four stages, with no significant decreases.

Analysis of these firms at the sub-regional level shows that they also represent higher shares in the Gulf countries than in the other MENA economies: From 27% to 49% of firms in Gulf economies; which is substantially higher than the 10% to 22% of the North West African and Middle East region firms.

Figure 2.8. **There is a significant larger share of firms oriented towards tourism and foreign markets in MENA than in other emerging countries**

Share of firms oriented towards tourism and foreign markets and by stage of business life course, 2009

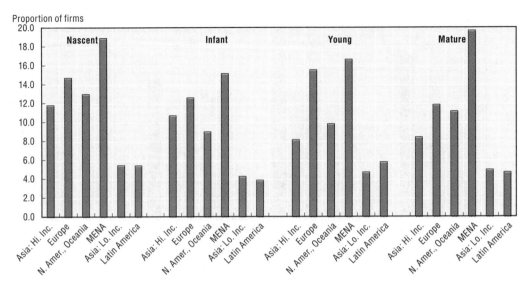

Notes:
Nascent: Profits for less than three months.
Infant: Profits for four months or 2.5 years.
Young: Profits for over 2.5 years and up to 5.5 years.
Mature: Profits for over 5.5 years.
Source: Reynolds (2013, forthcoming).

MENA economies compare well or very well with other emerging economies in terms of high potential firms

The analysis of high-potential enterprises provides some relevant insights. Importantly, that the MENA region is at no major disadvantage compared to other emerging economies. Actually, the average percentages of high-potential enterprises over the four stages of the business life course are generally higher in MENA than in other emerging economies for the four proxy indicators. Furthermore, MENA registers even higher rates of high-potential enterprises than developed economies in terms of two indicators: market-impact enterprises and firms oriented towards tourism and foreign markets.

This, however, does not directly imply that there will be more high growth firms in MENA than in other regions. As highlighted above, MENA economies have lower enterprise prevalence rates than other emerging economies, and lower prevalence of formal firms than any other region in the world except sub-Saharan Africa. In other words, if fewer firms are being created and developed then there will be a smaller firm population from which high growth enterprises (and all enterprises in general) are born.

Furthermore, a more detailed analysis of the group of proxy indicators of high potential shows that, in MENA, firms expecting job growth (the most straightforward indicator of high-impact) represent a lower proportion of all firms than those measured with the other three proxy indicators.

When analysing high-potential enterprises at each of the four stages of the business life course, it is also evident that nascent and, importantly, mature firms appear to represent higher shares than infant and young ones. In the case of firms employing technical staff, their share falls significantly at the young stage. For firms expecting job growth and enterprises oriented towards tourism and foreign markets the share slightly falls at the infant and young stages. This is in line with the general trend of the overall enterprise population, which is skewed towards the youngest and the oldest firms.

The sub-regional analysis also shows that, although Gulf countries have lower rates of enterprise activity than North West African and Middle Eastern economies, they have comparatively higher rates of high-potential enterprises. In summary, the North West African countries (Algeria, Morocco, and Tunisia) have high prevalence of firms in all four life-course stages. There is a relative emphasis on transformative sectors, but a low proportion operating in sectors likely to employ workers with technical skills. The proportion of firms expecting to have an impact on the market is low to moderate.

The five Middle Eastern economies (Egypt, Jordan, Lebanon, Syria, and Palestinian Authority) have moderate levels of firm prevalence. There is a considerable emphasis on customer-oriented sectors and more enterprises operating in sectors likely to employ workers with technical skills. Market impact is expected to be low to moderate and a small proportion expects to grow.

The two Gulf countries (Saudi Arabia, the United Arab Emirates) have a very low prevalence of enterprises in all life course stages. There is a relative emphasis on transformative sectors and high proportions operate in sectors likely to employ workers with technical skills. Moderate to high proportions expect to have a market impact. A very high proportion reports expectations of job growth.

Caveats of the indicators of high-potential as predictors of high growth

With the data from the GEM it is not possible to discern any specific features of high-potential enterprises that are somehow peculiar to MENA economies. The GEM data does not allow for multiple factor control, and therefore it is not possible to know with certainty the proportion of high-potential firms that are at the same time high-job-growth firms.

While in some countries surveyed by the GEM the samples are large enough to provide a representative sample of the enterprise population to estimate the share of firms with several high-potential characteristics, for some economies, particularly in MENA, the samples are too small to provide reliable estimates of the prevalence of high-potential firms based on multiple indicators.

Finally, high potential does not necessarily translate into actual high growth. Perhaps most importantly, differences among high growth enterprises can be huge: a single high growth firm may have great effects in an entire economic sector and probably on an entire economy, while a number of growing, but not out-performing enterprises, may simply compensate for the flat or negative performance of all other enterprises. The results emerging from the company interviews presented in Chapter 3 will shed light on this subject.

Key features of MENA entrepreneurs

A variety of information is useful to establish the characteristics of those involved as owners and managers of businesses. This review begins with the motivation to undertake enterprise activity, followed by an analysis of the gender, age and educational attainment of entrepreneurs. The objective is to distil key features of entrepreneurs in the MENA region. The analysis in this section focuses on the general population of entrepreneurs, while Chapter 3 focuses specifically on entrepreneurs heading high growth enterprises.

Opportunity-driven entrepreneurship in MENA is higher than in other emerging economies

Figure 2.9 displays the **motivation** reported by entrepreneurs across economy groups and for different stages in the firm life course. Those reporting that they were pursuing a promising business opportunity are distinguished from those who said that they had "no better choices for work", or necessity-driven entrepreneurs.

Figure 2.9. **Opportunity-driven entrepreneurial activity is higher in MENA than in other emerging economies**

Owner's contextual motivation: World groups by firm life course stage

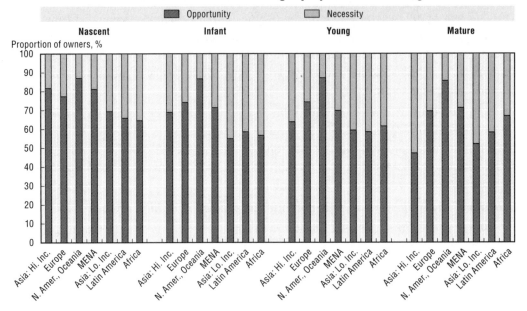

Notes:
Nascent: Profits for less than three months.
Infant: Profits for four months or 2.5 years.
Young: Profits for over 2.5 years and up to 5.5 years.
Mature: Profits for over 5.5 years.
Source: Reynolds (2013, forthcoming).

The popular image of business creation, however, tends to emphasise those voluntarily pursuing a promising business idea; there has been less attention to those with no better options. There are, however, differences in the types of firms developed and managed by opportunity and necessity owner-managers.

In the MENA region, more than three out of four new entrepreneurs are in business to pursue opportunities rather than by necessity or lack of other job prospects. This represents a higher share than in other emerging economies and is comparable to the share in developed economies. The share of opportunity-driven ventures remains relatively stable over the business life course, at 73% of the total, higher than all other emerging economies.

Two trends are clear from the GEM data. First, there is a general tendency for a larger proportion of business owners-managers in emerging economies to report they are involved out of necessity than in developed economies. Second, the proportion reporting they are involved out of necessity tends to increase further into the firm life course in emerging economies. The pattern across the MENA economies is typical of other emerging economy groups, but with fewer reports of necessity-driven entrepreneurship. There are also more opportunity-seeking entrepreneurs heading new than more established enterprises.

At the MENA sub-regional level and consistent with the pattern among world groups, the proportion of opportunity-based activity is highest among nascent entrepreneurs, where it is 80% in North West Africa to 90% in Gulf economies. These shares also decline for the infant, young, and mature firms.

The patterns associated with gender and age distribution highlight some more specific features of entrepreneurs in the MENA region.

Women-led enterprises in MENA represent a lower proportion than in other groups of countries

The gender distribution of entrepreneurship among different groups of economies is generally even, with women's representing about 35% of the firm owners in different firm life stages. However, the GEM (and other data sources) notes that the share of all ventures owned and managed by women is significantly lower in MENA than in the rest of the world. For instance, within the more restricted group of larger, registered firms in MENA that are surveyed annually by the World Bank Group, women account for only 13% of all enterprises (World Bank, 2010, page vii).

Higher rates of women-led nascent enterprises than of more mature enterprises can be due to a number of factors

A compounding factor in the overall difference between the situation in MENA and other regions is the relatively short lives of women's enterprises in the former: slightly more than 34% of all entrepreneurs in MENA heading a nascent enterprise are women, compared to 42% in other emerging economies. This proportion drops to 22% during the infant and young stages of the business life course, and continues decreasing to just 17% of mature firms, far lower than in other emerging and developed economies (Figure 2.10). On this basis, the IDRC *GEM-MENA Regional Report 2009* concluded that "the gender gap in entrepreneurial activity between male and female rates is narrowing" (IDRC, 2010, p. 17).

However, the situation in North West Africa skews the higher share of women among nascent entrepreneurs in MENA overall. There are marked variations across MENA countries in the rates of female involvement in entrepreneurial activity both in general (Bosma & Levie, 2010), across the business life cycle (Reynolds, 2013, forthcoming) and by age groups of individuals (IDRC, 2010). The *proportion* of women involved in nascent, compared to established ventures, is higher in the same country only in North West Africa[6] (IDRC, 2010).

It is worth noting that the share of women among the nascent firm owners in the North West African economies is particularly high, just below 50%, a share well comparable to that of other emerging economies in Latin America and Asia. This may indicate a major recent generational change, as the presence of women in infant and young firms in the North West African countries is similar to that in the other MENA sub-regions (Figure 2.11). On the other hand, as shown in Figure 2.11, women have a marginal role in managing-owning well-established firms in the Gulf countries, but even more so in the Middle East economies.

Figure 2.10. **MENA has fewer women entrepreneurs than other emerging and low-income countries, but within the region there are more women entrepreneurs leading enterprises in the earlier business stages than more established enterprises**

Firm owner's gender: World groups by firm life course stage

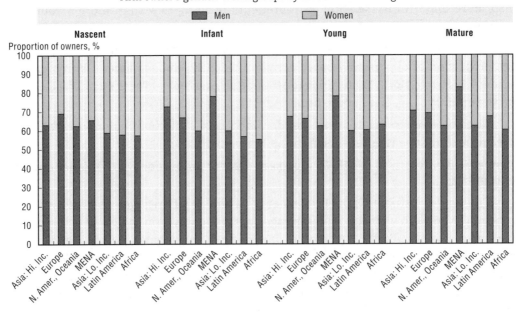

Notes:

Nascent: Profits for less than three months.
Infant: Profits for four months or 2.5 years.
Young: Profits for over 2.5 years and up to 5.5 years.
Mature: Profits for over 5.5 years.

Source: Reynolds (2013, forthcoming).

Figure 2.11. **The share of women leading nascent firms is higher in the North West Africa sub-region than in the other MENA sub-regions**

Firm owner's gender: MENA groups by firm life course stage

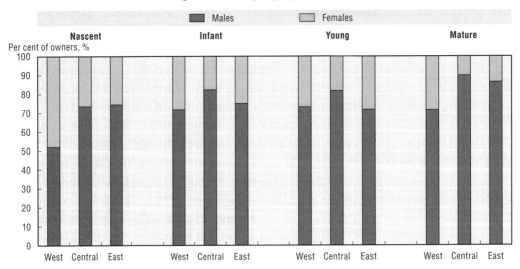

Notes:

Nascent: Profits for less than three months.
Infant: Profits for four months or 2.5 years.
Young: Profits for over 2.5 years and up to 5.5 years.
Mature: Profits for over 5.5 years.

Source: Reynolds (2013, forthcoming).

Even that precise observation cannot be assumed to indicate a change in North West Africa in women's behaviour, *i.e.* it does not show a change over time in women's propensity to undertake entrepreneurial activity (although it *may do so*).[7] Rates of entrepreneurial activity are already notably higher for both men and women in North West Africa compared to the Middle East and the Gulf. The rate of early stage entrepreneurship among men is approximately 19% in North West Africa, 11% in the Middle East and 7% in the Gulf, whereas rates among women are 9%, 5% and 3.5%, respectively (Bosma and Levie, 2010, and Hattab, 2009).

The ratio of women to male entrepreneurs is correlated with gender differences in participation in the labour market. Women's participation in the MENA labour market remains well below that of other regions. On average, a mere 32% of working-age women join the labour force in the MENA region, compared to 56% in emerging economies and 61% in OECD countries (OECD-World Economic Forum, 2011). There has been an increase in the rate over the last ten years (World Bank, 2012). This finding might support the suggestion that women's entrepreneurial activity rates in MENA may, indeed, have been rising, but the evidence is inconclusive.

Women in MENA are more active as entrepreneurs than as labour force participants

Whatever the dynamics of the situation, and although the gender difference in entrepreneurial activity rates is striking, in fact women in the MENA region are considerably more active as entrepreneurs than as participants in the labour force, as conventionally measured.[8] While men are twice as likely as women to be involved in business, they are between two and a half and three and a half times more likely than women to participate in the labour force (Table 2.2).[9]

Table 2.2. **Ratios of male/female activity rates in the labour force and in entrepreneurial activity**

	MENA average	North West Africa	Central	East
Labour force participation	2.9:1	2.5:1	3.5:1	2.7:1
Entrepreneurial activity	2.1:1	2.1:1	2.2:1	2.0:1

Sources: Calculated from World Bank Indicators, Bosma and Levie, 2010, and Hattab, 2009.

Women entrepreneurs lead younger firms, have lower levels of education, shorter job experience than men and operate their businesses mostly in consumer services

Women's ventures are younger and less established than men's ventures in MENA. The proportion of ventures owned and managed by women is lower, the older and more established is the enterprise.

However, within each age class of firms, the GEM data show few significant differences between the types of ventures owned and managed by women and men in MENA in respect of the resources (human, financial, etc.) within the firm. The data allow differences within only two age classes of enterprise to be considered with confidence: "nascent" and "young and mature" ventures.

According to the GEM data, women owner-managers of nascent ventures have less education (although more than the female population on average) and very much less employment experience than men.

Female entrepreneurs are of similar age to men, and they share similar levels of readiness for entrepreneurship, fear of failure, income levels of their households, motivations for starting their businesses and opinion of the supportiveness of the business environment.

There is no gender difference among nascent entrepreneurs in the owners' assessment of the newness of their product offering. Only slightly greater prospects are seen by male entrepreneurs for the growth of the business in terms of the future number of jobs to be created or the share of exports to be attained, and in numbers of highly technically qualified staff employed.

There is a major gender difference in the sector of engagement. Relatively speaking, many more women operate in consumer services, as opposed to extractive or transformative industries or business services.

Among more established (young and mature) businesses, the comparison narrows even further. The women owner/managers of these types of firms are similar to male owner/managers in personal attributes (age, engagement in other work, (high) levels of readiness for entrepreneurship, (low) fear of failure, level of household income, and "pull" motivations for starting their businesses and in their opinion of the supportiveness of the business environment.

In terms of the characteristics of their ventures, there is a narrowing of difference by gender with respect to many factors, including, the newness of their product offering, perceived prospects for the growth of the business in terms of the future number of jobs to be created or the share of exports to be attained.

As with nascent enterprises, however, male owner/managers of more established ventures are somewhat more likely to operate with technically qualified staff. The difference in the sector of engagement persists, with higher proportion of women's ventures in consumer services as their line of business.

All these differences (lower education and job experience, growth expectations, concentration in consumer services, etc.) could lead one to *assume* that there would be lower numbers of high-impact enterprises led by women.

However, a study of the gender characteristics of registered enterprises in eight MENA countries[10] comes to a different conclusion. It shows that the widely held perception that the few female entrepreneurs in the Middle East and North West Africa region are mainly in the micro sector (employing fewer than 10 workers), producing less sophisticated goods and services, is wrong. Of the formal-sector female-owned firms surveyed, only 8% are micro firms. More than 30% are very large firms employing more than 250 workers. The distribution by firm size is very similar among female and male-owned formal firms across the region (World Bank, 2010, pages vii-viii).[11]

The same study also shows that female-owned firms, in fact, perform as well as – or in some cases better than – male-owned firms in a number of other dimensions, such as, exporting, share of foreign investors, use of information technology, and the quality of jobs they offer and skills they require in their workforce. Moreover, "female-owned firms are hiring more workers in general. In Egypt, Jordan, Saudi Arabia, and the West Bank and Gaza, the share of female-owned firms that have increased their workforces recently exceeds the share of male-owned firms" (World Bank, 2010, page viii).

The seemingly contradictory evidence from the GEM data and the World Bank study points to the need for a more in-depth research of women-led high potential- and high-impact enterprises.

Possible determinants of the reduction in the share of women's enterprises in successive age classes of firms

Information on the similarity of firm characteristics and performance seems to point towards factors in the operating environment as the cause, rather than factors integral to the enterprise or the competencies of the entrepreneur herself.

Reynolds' (2013, forthcoming) analysis of the factors associated with the relatively low rate of creation of new enterprises and the apparently higher rates of closure of women's ventures in MENA suggests that one overwhelmingly important factor is at play: the low rate of female participation in the labour force.

In MENA, the majority of entrepreneurs report being in employment, and within the population as a whole, early-stage entrepreneurship rates are highest for adults who are already working either full- or part-time (IDRC, 2010). Thus, the fact that relatively few women are participating in the labour force in MENA has the secondary effect of holding back the propensity of women to undertake entrepreneurial activity in the region as a whole.

However, the low rate of female labour-force participation would seem to be most relevant at the earliest stage of enterprise formation. It has less direct effect on later stages of business,[12] although there is a secondary effect in that prevalence depends on presence in the precursor (nascent) stages. The prevalence of work experience among MENA women owner/managers of established businesses is very similar to the level of work experience among women entrepreneurs at the same stage in other parts of the world (Reynolds, 2013, forthcoming, Table 10).

The low numbers of women entrepreneurs in MENA at later stages of the firm life cycle could be due to factors in either the business or the social environment, or both. This calls for further analysis.

With respect to the business operating environment, the GEM database does not reveal any differences by gender in entrepreneurs' perception of the impact of the business environment. The World Bank report cited above also argues that the business environment in the Middle East and North West Africa region is not itself systematically gendered. However, it suggests that women's weaker status (indeed their "minor" legal status) in other areas of the law affecting, for example, personal mobility, may impinge on their ability to run a business (World Bank, 2010).

Women's generally lower access to personal assets could reduce their ability to offer collateral and thus hinder their access to finance for their business. In a study of gender-based differences among workers and entrepreneurs in Lebanon, differences were found between male and female entrepreneurs in terms of access to finance, as measured by both the demand for finance and the kind of financial instruments used (World Bank, 2009).

Social norms might seem more constraining in relation to business creation, rather than to the continuing operation of women's businesses. Nevertheless, social norms could come into play for women who marry and become mothers, perhaps leading them to withdraw from entrepreneurial activity for family reasons. However, the age distribution of women in nascent and established businesses in MENA is not skewed towards young and middle aged (as opposed to prime age) women. There is no divergence from the age profile of women entrepreneurs in other parts of the world, and no difference from the age distribution of male entrepreneurs in MENA.

GEM data offer one slight clue to the possible cause of women's relatively low rates of entrepreneurial activity. In response to a question about the reasons for discontinuation in a previous business, "men and women are equally likely to report problems getting finance, but women [are] (…) less likely to report they left the business because it was not profitable (35% versus 45% of men)." Second, women are more likely to report personal reasons (29% of women versus 22% of men)" (IDRC 2010: 53). This difference is, however, not strongly compelling evidence that family responsibilities are a strong determinant of the low prevalence of women's entrepreneurial activity rates in MENA. The issue needs further investigation.

Younger entrepreneurs manage younger firms

Looking at the age distribution across the business life stages, across all the regional groups the share of older entrepreneurs is particularly high in mature firms.

Those under 35 years of age are, on average, 54% of the nascent firm owners in all groups of countries, ranging from 42% in developed Asia to over 61% in MENA. On the other hand, nascent firm owners/managers aged 45 and older represent on average only 20% of all owners in all groups of countries. Conversely, mature enterprise owners/managers aged 45 and more represent higher shares (on average 47%) than those aged 18-34 years (on average 22%). As noted in Figure 2.12, there is a clear pattern in the data developed from international comparisons: there are more older owners among the more established enterprises (young and mature) compared to the newer (nascent and infant) ventures.

In addition, emerging economies and lower income countries have a substantially higher proportion of younger enterprise owners at all stages of the firm life course, probably reflecting both the swelling population of younger individuals and/or the lack of job opportunities for younger people.

This is also the case for the MENA region. Again, as in the case of gender, it is not possible to assess, based simply on this set of GEM data, if a generation change is taking place or simply that less-experienced entrepreneurs have lower chances to have their business survive. The following section, which focuses on education attainment, gives further elements of analysis.

At the sub-regional level within MENA, the GEM data indicates that young adults, 18-34 years of age, are 60% of the nascent firm owner-managers in the North West Africa and Middle East sub-regions, but those 45-64 years of age are 40-45% of the owner managers of mature firms. In the Gulf countries, however, those 45-64 years of age are 45% of the nascent firm owner managers and this figure increases to almost 70% for owner managers of mature firms. Among all GEM countries, it is unusual to have such a high proportion of older individuals involved in all stages of the business life course.

MENA entrepreneurs appear to have higher levels of educational attainment

GEM data show that entrepreneurs in the MENA region have, on average, higher levels of education attainment than in other emerging economies. As shown in Figure 2.13, over 22% of entrepreneurs running nascent firms in MENA have a post-secondary degree (13-16 years of schooling), similar to the share in Latin America and higher than in emerging Asia (18%) and Africa (14%). The share is higher for owner-managers with graduate degrees (17-20 years

Figure 2.12. **Across all the regional groups, the share of older entrepreneurs is higher in mature firms**

Firm owner's age: World groups by firm life course stage

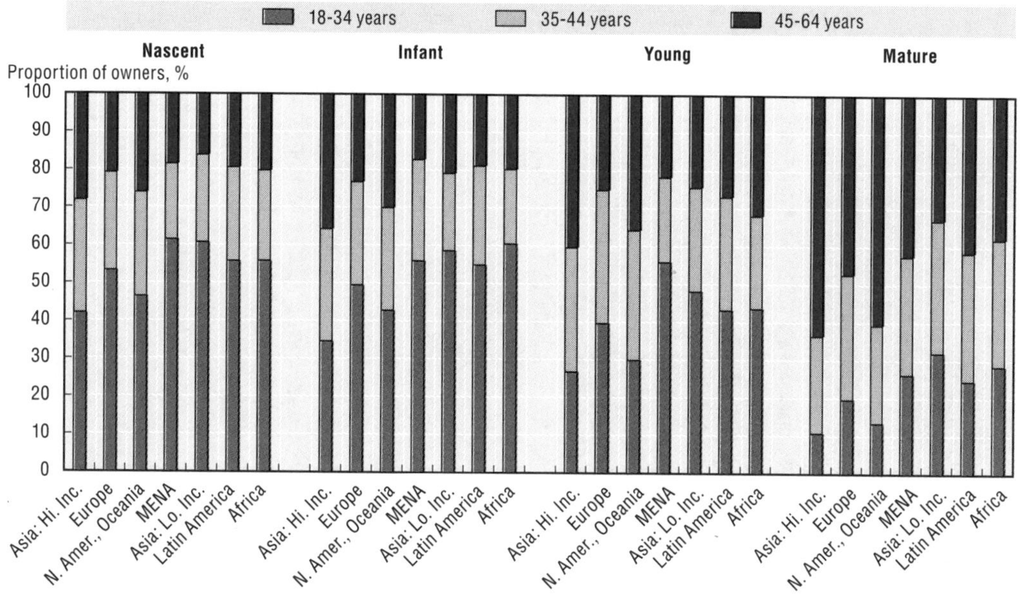

Notes:

Nascent: Profits for less than three months.

Infant: Profits for four months or 2.5 years.

Young: Profits for over 2.5 years and up to 5.5 years.

Mature: Profits for over 5.5 years.

Source: Reynolds (2013, forthcoming).

of schooling): 18% in MENA compared to 13% in emerging Asia, 10% in Latin America and nearly 6% in Africa. This may be the result of either higher general levels of education in some MENA economies (e.g. Jordan and Tunisia) and/or a higher propensity among the more educated towards entrepreneurship.

Again, the issue of how to read cross-sectional data in a dynamic way arises. It would be reasonable to assume that enterprises headed by graduates have at least the same chances to survive as enterprises set up by less-educated entrepreneurs, and therefore the higher share of more-educated entrepreneurs in the early enterprises business stages is an indication of generational change.

Are enterprises that are led by more-educated entrepreneurs higher performing than those headed by less-educated entrepreneurs? The GEM data cannot answer this question, but inputs from the virtual focus group analysed in Chapter 3 may shed more light on the relationship between an entrepreneur's educational attainment and enterprise performance.

At the MENA sub-regional level, half or more of owner-managers at all life course stages have not completed secondary school in the North West African countries. For the Middle East Region economies, the distribution of educational attainment does not vary much across the firm life course, 20-30% of the entrepreneurs have not completed secondary school, 20-30% have completed secondary school, and about half have post-secondary school experience.

Figure 2.13. **Entrepreneurs in MENA have a higher level of educational attainment than in other emerging economies**

Owner educational attainment: World groups by firm life course stage

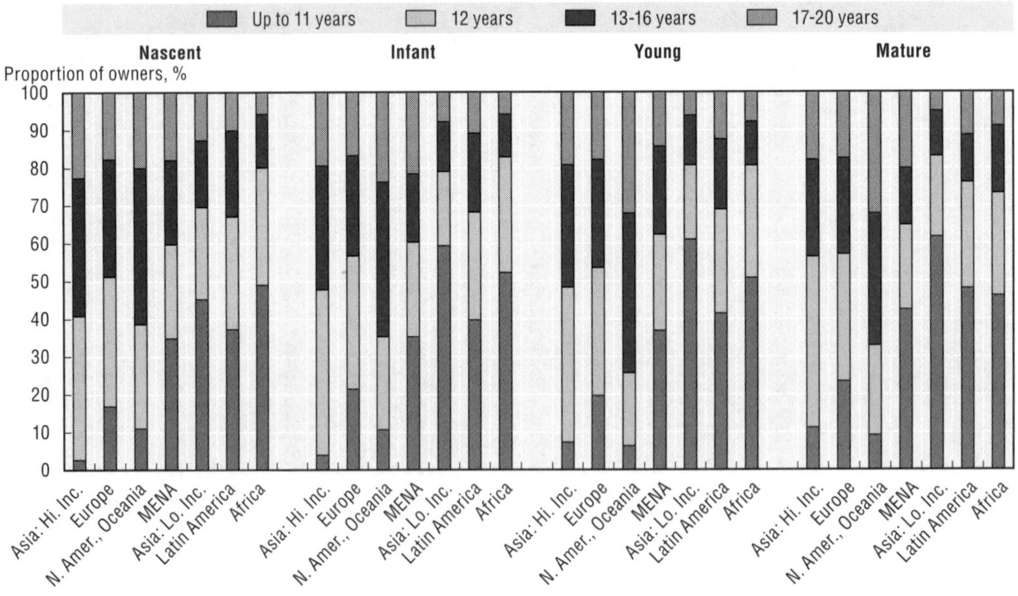

Notes:
Nascent: Profits for less than three months.
Infant: Profits for four months or 2.5 years.
Young: Profits for over 2.5 years and up to 5.5 years.
Mature: Profits for over 5.5 years.
Source: Reynolds (2013, forthcoming).

The pattern of educational attainment for different firm life course stages in the Gulf countries is very particular: educational attainment is much higher at all stages of the firm life course, with over half of those in the nascent stage reporting graduate training and only about 10% in all stages reporting they had not completed secondary school.

Summing up observations of key features of enterprises and entrepreneurs in the region

The key features coming out of the previous sections are:

Enterprise prevalence in different stages of the business life course

- enterprise creation and development in MENA is lower than in emerging economies (and in all economies, except Sub-Saharan Africa, if only formal firms are considered). In other words, fewer firms being created and developed results in a smaller firm population from which high growth enterprises (and all enterprises in general) are drawn; and

- at the sub-regional level, entrepreneurial activity in North West Africa is comparable to other emerging economies and significantly higher than in Gulf countries over the four stages of the business life course.

Sectors of economic activity in the different stages of the business life course

- MENA economies register lower shares of firms in (higher value added) business services activities and higher shares in customer-oriented activities;

- enterprises in business services may face important challenges in the consolidation of their activity when they reach 2.5-5.5 years of existence; and

- within MENA, Middle Eastern economies register lower levels of business services and transformative firms than North African and Gulf economies.

The prevalence of firms with "high potential"

Firms in sectors likely to employ staff with comparatively high technical skills

- GEM data shows that this type of high-potential firm represents a higher average in MENA than in other emerging economies over the four stages of the business life course;

- their share in MENA is relatively steady during the first two stages of the business life course, but it falls from nascent to infant, which suggests that many of those firms do not survive the first 2.5 years;

- this may indicate that these firms have greater rates of survival during the first 2.5 years of their lives in the case of the MENA region, but they seem to face hurdles to survival between 2.5 and 5.5 years of existence;

- mature firms in sectors likely to employ staff with high technical skills represent a higher share in MENA than in the other groups of countries; and

- the sub-regional analysis of GEM data indicates that North African economies have lower shares of high-potential firms employing staff with technical skills than the other two MENA sub-regions.

Market impact firms

- Firms expecting to have an impact on the markets in which they operate are significantly higher in MENA than in any other group of economies. This may reflect the rapid transformation of customer-oriented sectors of MENA economies, as new customers in MENA encounter retail and service businesses familiar to customers in developed countries.

- Market-impact firms also register high shares within all three MENA sub-regions, especially in the Gulf sub-region, where they average a quarter of all firms in the first two stages of the business life course and over 30% during the young and mature stages. The proportion of firms expecting to have an impact in the markets is lowest for the Middle Eastern region among nascent, young and mature firms; there is no regional intraregional difference for infant firms.

Firms expecting job growth

- The MENA region does not appear to have any specific disadvantage compared to other emerging economies in terms of firms expecting to create 20 or more jobs over the next five years.

- The share of firms expecting job growth in MENA is relatively steady over the business life course (around 8%) and slightly higher in the mature stage (10%). This is a comparatively higher share than in other emerging economies and similar to that of the developed economies in Europe and North America-Oceania. There is not a very significant difference between mature and nascent firms (9%).

- At the sub-regional level, firms expecting job growth are a significantly higher proportion in Gulf countries than in other MENA economies, which indicates that the MENA average is pushed upwards by these countries, without which the overall MENA share would be even lower.

Firms oriented towards tourism and foreign markets

- As in the case of market-impact firms, enterprises oriented towards tourism and foreign markets represent a larger share in MENA than in all other economies, and a very significant higher share than in emerging economies.

- Furthermore, the share is importantly higher than in all groups of economies in the mature stage, which means that firms oriented towards tourism and exports are rather well established.

- When analysing the percentages of firms across different stages in the business life course, it is possible to see that although the trends are similar to those of enterprise prevalence in general, with more firms in the nascent and mature stages, their overall shares remain stable over the four stages, with no significant decreases.

- At the sub-regional level, these firms represent also significantly higher shares in Gulf economies than in the rest of MENA.

Insights from high potential firms

- The average percentages of high-potential enterprises over the four stages of the business life course in MENA are comparable to other emerging economies for the four proxy indicators. Furthermore, MENA registers even higher rates of high-potential enterprises than developed economies in terms of two indicators: market-impact enterprises and firms oriented towards tourism and foreign markets.

- This, however, does not directly imply that there will be more high growth enterprises in MENA than in other regions. As highlighted above, MENA economies have lower enterprise prevalence rates than other emerging economies, and lower prevalence of formal firms than any other region in the world except sub-Saharan Africa. In other words, if fewer firms are being created and developed then there will be a smaller firm population from which high growth enterprises (and all enterprises in general) are born.

What are the main factors behind business creation?

The following section analyses a set of factors associated with business creation. The aim of the analysis is to focus progressively on the influence of the business environment on business creation and business development. In particular, the section identifies the key elements of an enabling business environment and analyses general and specific factors.

Methodological approach

The methodology used to identify key factors associated with business creation consists of running a number of linear regressions, using enterprise prevalence rates of **nascent ventures and new firms** per 100 adults aged 18-64[13] as the dependent variable and testing the casual impact of different set of factors (listed in Table 2.3).

Regressions were made for the 75 countries covered by the GEM, using averages for the period 2000-2009 for which data was available. There is substantial variation in the number of years a country or economy is included in the dataset, from one to ten years. As the year-to-year variation in prevalence rates is relatively small compared to variation among countries, the average values for all years for which data was available was averaged to represent each country. Further methodological details are provided in Reynolds (2013, forthcoming).

A few factors appear to be significantly associated with business creation

Twenty-four factors or national characteristics thought to have a causal impact on business creation ("predictors") were utilised in the development of the regression models (examined in Reynolds, 2011 and 2013, forthcoming).[14] Those factors are listed in Table 2.3, which shows that six factors account for 84% of the variation in the prevalence of **nascent ventures** and seven factors account for 93% of the variation in the prevalence of **new firms**. This provides strong confidence that major national factors associated with these **first two stages** of the business life course are identified and that are useful to characterise groups of similar countries in terms of factors associated with business creation.

Those factors listed below are in order of importance:

1. "**Traditional values**" reflect a strong emphasis on self-reliance, responsibility for the economic wellbeing of the household, and a reluctance to expect help from government sources;

2. The **prevalence of informal investors** among the adult population reflects the capacity to acquire funds during the start-up phase and a supportive climate for business creation;

3. **Readiness for entrepreneurial careers** among the adult population, based on an index reflecting perception of business opportunities, confidence in skills to start a business, and knowing other entrepreneurs. In other words, this factor measures an individual's confidence in the prospects for success with a new business;

4. A reduced **level of population growth** over the period 1999-2009, which is interpreted as producing fewer young adults in the total population, which may reduce the perception of competition for a new firm from age peers by candidates for nascent entrepreneurship;

5. A greater **proportion of women and men participating in the labour force** translates into more individuals with skills and in a position to identify promising business opportunities. Reynolds (2011) displays the indicators for women and men separately.

None of the measures relates to either the structural features of the economy or the level of centralised control of economic activity (as shown in the empty cells in Table 2.3).

Low shares of women in the workforce are translated into low levels of enterprise creation

Two results from the regressions, in particular, were unexpected. The first is the lack of impact of one of the main measures of economic development, GDP per capita. As both the emphasis on traditional values and the proportion of men and women in the labour force (even if unemployed), are associated with lower GDP per capita, these factors may have a more consistent independent relationship with the prevalence of nascent ventures.

Perhaps most unexpected is the indication that annual population growth, once other factors are taken into account, has a negative relationship with the prevalence of nascent ventures. The general expectation would be that population growth would increase the demand for goods and services and, in turn, provide new business opportunities. However, the regressions show a negative correlation between average population growth and the proportion of women active in the labour force. In other words, the higher the average population growth, the fewer women are working. Consequently, two variables in the prediction of nascent venture prevalence reflect the roles of women in the national social structure, which represents a very striking finding.

Table 2.3. **Linear Regression Model: Nascent ventures and new firms**

		Nascent	New firm
	Number of countries	75.0	74.0
	Per cent variance explained (R * R)	83.0	93.1
Constant	[Standardised beta coefficient in cells]	−.63	−.99
Economic characteristics			
	GDP per capita (PPP): 2009: $1-$16 000/YR		
	GDP per capita (PPP): 2009: $16-$35 000/YR	Base	Base
	GDP per capita (PPP): 2009: $35-$57 000/YR		−.29
	Per cent change GDP per capita: 2003-08		
	Average annual pop. growth: 1999-2009	−.33	
	Income inequality: 2000-2008 average		
Structural features of the economy			
	New firms/100 persons 18-64 years old		NA[2]
	Established firms/100 persons 18-64 years old		0.59
	Percentage of agricultural workers: 2009		
	Percentage of industrial workers: 2009	Base[1]	Base
	Percentage of service workers: 2009		
Centralised control of economic activity			
	Percentage of government workers		
	Government spending as a percentage of GDP		
	Business start regulation index (ratio)		
	Costs for commercial legal action index		−.38
	Physical property rights recognition index		
	Intellectual property rights recognition index		
	Perceived corruption index: 2005		
Population capacity for business creation			
	National index: Readiness for entrepreneurship	0.44	0.15
	Percentage of total population 25-44 years old		
	Percentage HS degree or more 15+ years		
	Percentage of women 15-64 years old in labour force: 2007	0.25	0.36
	Percentage of men 15-64 years old in labour force: 2007	0.17	0.14
	Average unemployment rate: 2000-2008		
National cultural and social support			
	Prevalence informal investors: #/100 persons	0.49	
	National index of support for entrepreneurship		
	Traditional vs. secular/rational values emphasis	0.65	0.31
	Survival vs self-expressive values		

1. Base for comparisons not included in the regression analysis.
2. Not included in this regression analysis.
Note: New firms are those reporting profits for up to 3.5 years. The group includes all nascent and infant enterprises and part of the young enterprises (operating firms with profits from 31 to 66 months). Empty cells indicate that some of the factors did not provide independent contributions to improve the capacity to predict the level of participation in business creation. Further details are provided in Reynolds (2013, forthcoming).
Source: Reynolds (2013, forthcoming).

This is very relevant because the proportion of women working and the average population growth are two indicators of the extent to which women are (or are not) involved in work and part of the pool of potential nascent entrepreneurs. Hence, the fewer women there are in the work force, the fewer women there are that will develop business skills, find themselves in situations that will lead to the recognition of business opportunities, or know others that are involved in business creation.

From this analysis, and subject to the qualifications specified in Reynolds (2011)[15] a start-up nascent venture creation factors "scorecard" is presented for the three groups of economies, developed, emerging and MENA, in Figure 2.14.

Figure 2.14. **The low levels of women in employment appear to be a key factor for low enterprise creation in MENA**

Factors associated with nascent ventures: Three global country groups compared

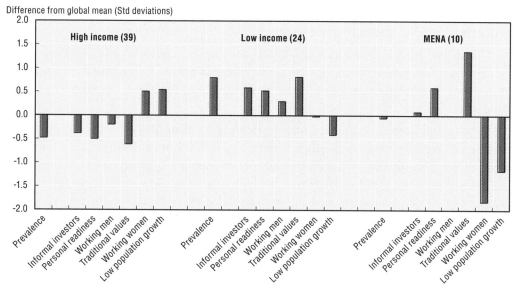

Source: Reynolds (2013, forthcoming).

For this assessment, all national characteristics, including the nascent and new firm prevalence rates, are normalised across the 75 countries to have an average value of zero and a standard deviation of 1.0.[16] Each country, therefore, is represented in terms of its relationship to the average values for all 75 countries. In this assessment, all countries are given equal weight, regardless of substantial differences in the size of human and business populations.[17]

In addition, the values are adjusted so that a positive value represents a positive association with firm creation and a negative value a negative association. For example, a positive value on traditional values would indicate a strong emphasis on traditional values and a reduced emphasis on secular-rational values. A positive value on low population growth would reflect low population growth, associated with greater business creation; a negative value would represent higher population growth which is associated with less business creation.

The profile of MENA economies appears on the right side of Figure 2.14. It shows that the prevalence of participation in nascent ventures is about average for the 75 countries, intermediate between the developed and emerging economy groups presented in Table 2.1 above.

On three measures, there is one significant difference for MENA economies. The labour-force participation of women is almost two standard deviations below the global average and the emphasis on traditional values is more than a standard deviation above the global average. This is, compared to the other regions, a unique combination of factors. The high level of population growth, compared to other countries, would also reduce the prevalence of participation in start-up activity.

As noted above, the MENA region has a significantly lower share of women entrepreneurs than other emerging economies. Now it is possible to link this specific feature directly to the lower participation of women in the labour market. A very large share of entrepreneurs starts a business after having accumulated relevant work experience. Employment contributes to the accumulation of skills, identifying potential business opportunities and to setting aside financial resources to start a business. Therefore, a lower share of women in employment in MENA compared with other country groups means that the pool from which the new entrepreneurs are likely to emerge is from the beginning smaller than in other regions.

The higher impact of traditional values in MENA compared with other country groups most likely reflects the high presence of those values in the MENA countries. It may also be an indication of the prevalence of family businesses and the high importance of mutual trust in business relations.

Finally, the negative influence of population growth in MENA on the nascent-firms prevalence rate, compared with other country groups, indicates that the rate of business creation is not keeping up with the very high rate of population growth. All MENA countries are in a phase of demographic transition, with population growth rates of over 2% per year during the 2000s, compared with an average of 0.5% in OECD countries. Very high population growth tends to outstrip the potential for job creation of an economy in the short to medium term. The results are higher unemployment and under-employment as the main avenue leading to enterprise creation.

The same assessment applies to the prevalence of new firms, defined as those reporting profits for up to 3.5 years. For this assessment, seven national factors account for 93% of the variation in the prevalence of new firms. Several of these factors are similar to those reported for nascent enterprises.[18]

Table 2.4 provides an overview of the major differences found among the MENA region in these factors.

Table 2.4. **Overview of MENA region factors related to business creation**

National characteristics	Nascent	New firm
Prevalence	Global average	Global average
Informal investors	Global average	
Personal readiness for entrepreneurship	Slightly above	
Proportion of working women	Very much below	
Traditional values emphasis	Much higher	
Low population growth	High population growth	
Small business prevalence		Slightly above
Personal readiness for entrepreneurship		Slightly above
Income inequality		Slightly above
Percentage of young adults		Slightly above
Percentage of working women		Very much below
Percentage of high school graduates		Slightly below
Low unemployment rate		Slightly below

Source: Reynolds (2013, forthcoming).

Figure 2.15 shows the factors associated with business creation at the MENA sub-regional level. It shows that the prevalence of nascent ventures is above the global average for the North West African countries region, while slightly below for the Middle East economies, and much below average for the Gulf countries. A high existing prevalence rate, calculated over the whole enterprise population, is generally positively correlated with business creation. Since GEM data gathers information on both formal and informal firms, it is not possible to say that this may be an indication that the business environment is conducive to the establishment and survival of new enterprises.

The prevalence of women in the labour force is much below the global average in all MENA regions, but the difference is greatest in the Middle East sub-region. This again highlights the correlation between relatively limited participation of women in the labour market, implying a lower accumulation of experience, information on business opportunities and financial resources, and a lower than predicted rate of enterprise creation. Those observations are very much influenced by the data inputs from Egypt, which is the most populous and the largest economy in the Middle East sub-region.

Combined female participation, prevalence rate and high population growth may explain much of the significant difference in the number of enterprises per adults between the North West African and the Middle East sub-regions noted above. In other terms, as the labour-market participation rate among North West African women is higher on average than in the Middle East countries, more women may be in a position to start a new enterprise.

A partly different dynamic seems to apply to the Gulf countries. The inverse relation between population growth and enterprise creation has already been mentioned. What is peculiar in these countries is the relationship between women's participation in the labour force and enterprise creation.

Linking data on women's presence among enterprise owners and managers with factors influencing enterprise creation shows that, while the low participation rates of women in the labour force in the Gulf countries have a negative impact on company creation, compared to North West African countries, the presence of women entrepreneurs in the Gulf is much lower across all the business stages. This may imply that the correlation between women in employment and the rate of business creation in the Gulf countries is weaker than in the other two MENA sub-regions.

Figure 2.15. There are some key differences in terms of factors behind enterprise creation within the MENA region

Factors associated with nascent ventures: Three MENA regions compared

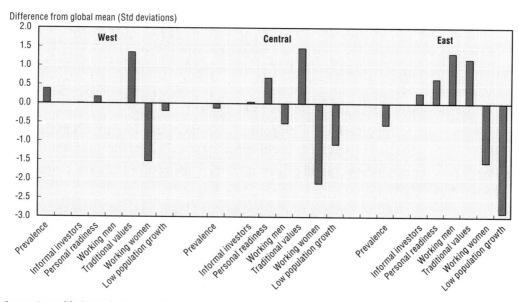

Source: Reynolds (2013, forthcoming).

The role of public policy in fostering enterprise creation

Public policy can influence some factors, such as population growth and the proportion of young adults in the labour force, only with difficulty. Others, such as a strong emphasis on traditional values, are already at a high level compared to other countries. Others, such as the prevalence of small businesses and the unemployment rate, relate to the structure of the economy and may be affected by greater public participation in business creation. Public policies or programmes could influence several factors in the medium term, particularly the level of educational attainment in the population and personal readiness for entrepreneurship. It is possible that greater participation in educational programmes and entrepreneurship training schemes could do much to improve personal readiness for entrepreneurship.

The major distinctive factor, reducing the level of MENA business creation, is the low participation of women in the world of work. As this appears to reflect well-established cultural norms, it may be the most difficult to change, but may be the factor with the greatest potential for impact on MENA business creation.

Evidence from the MENA-OECD Investment Programme's Working Group on SME Policy, Entrepreneurship and Human Capital Development indicates that the limited development of entrepreneurship in MENA can be explained by at least three factors: 1) high barriers to doing business, particularly for smaller firms (e.g. corruption, complex licenses, rigid labour laws and unfair competition); 2) cultural norms in which entrepreneurial activity is seen by young graduates as second-best compared with employment in the public sector, which offers better job security; and 3) the very low participation of women in the labour force and in entrepreneurial activity (OECD-World Economic Forum, 2011).

Summary and conclusions

This chapter concludes by highlighting the similarities and the differences among MENA countries in relation to business creation.

When compared to six other groups of countries, the MENA countries:

- Have a prevalence of new and profitable firms that is intermediate between high-income and European countries and low-income countries.
- Have a total amount of business activity that is much less than in low-income Asian countries, less than in Latin American countries, but comparable to countries in Europe or North America/Oceania and more than in high-income Asian countries.
- Have a proportion of firms in different economic sectors comparable to that in other low-income countries.

The owner-managers in the MENA countries appear to:

- Be responding to opportunities in proportions typical of low-income countries, with slightly more reporting involvement out of necessity than in high-income countries.
- Have fewer women involved at all stages of the firm life course than any of the other groups of countries.
- Have a larger proportion of young adults, 18-34 years of age, involved in the early stages of the business life course - nascent, infant, and young - than any other country group.
- Have both a high proportion of individuals who have not completed secondary education involved in businesses similar to that in other low-income countries and a high proportion with graduate experience in the nascent and infant stages, similar to that in high-income countries.

- Have a slightly lower proportion, but still a majority, of nascent ventures initiated by those with full or part time work.

The major policy implications vary for these different characteristics:

- It is clear that women are more involved in the nascent stages than in the later firm stages in all sub-regions. This may reflect either a problem with women turning nascent ventures into profitable new firms or a greater acceptance of younger women in the business world.

- The age pattern of enterprising individuals in the North West Africa and Middle East sub-regions is broadly typical of all world regions, in that younger people are more active in start-ups, while the owners of profitable mature firms tend to be older. The high proportion of older adults involved in the nascent stage in the Gulf sub-region is distinctive and perhaps policies to encourage more young adults to participate in the start-up phase would lead to more business creation.

- The higher level of education among owners of profitable firms, particularly in the North West Africa and Middle East sub-regions, compared with those operating nascent ventures, may reflect the advantages of education. It suggests that completion of secondary (or high) school provides some advantage in the business creation process.

- The higher levels of household income associated with later stages of the firm life course suggests that a benefit to those that manage to create a profitable firm is that their household income may increase.

- All MENA regions reflect the universal pattern related to labour-force status at the time of participating in the start-up phase of the firm life course. The majority of individuals have a job when then engage in the business-creation process. This is somewhat lower in the North West Africa sub-region, which may reflect higher levels of unemployment.

Notes

1. There are over 3 nascent ventures and almost 4 mature firms for each 100 adults (age range 18-64), compared to only 2 infant firms and young firms.

2. Entrepreneurship that creates jobs, societal wealth, and improvements in standards of living.

3. Data on firm growth is available for some OECD member and non-member countries through the Entrepreneurship Indicators Programme database (see OECD, 2011, pp. 73-79). There is no data available for the MENA region.

4. Based on the procedure developed by Hecker (2005 – as cited by Reynolds, 2013, forthcoming); a summary of the sectors is provided in Appendix B of Reynolds (2011 – also cited by Reynolds, 2013, forthcoming).

5. For nascent firms the basis is 25% of expected customers residing in foreign countries. Tourism revenues are not distinguished from other export revenues in the data.

6. And within that region predominantly within only one country (Algeria).

7. The GEM data does not preclude the possibility that such an increase may in fact be taking place, either in North Africa or elsewhere in the MENA region.

8. According to ILO definitions of the labour force, as including paid and unpaid family workers, as well as people actively seeking such work, measured in the same way across countries. Feminist scholars, who draw attention to women's much greater contribution to the unpaid "care" economy, dispute this definition of economic activity.

9. There is some double counting, in that entrepreneurially active women are equally participating in the labour force (especially in respect of more established ventures); taking account of this factor would widen the differential between the two ratios.

10. Morocco, Algeria, Tunisia, Egypt, Jordan, Lebanon, WBGS and Yemen.

11. Nevertheless, the size distribution of all ventures (such as covered in the GEM project, although precise data on the size of ventures is not included in the GEM database) could differ by gender. There may be an association, for example, between the unusually high female entrepreneurial activity rate in Morocco (IDRC, 2010) and the much higher share of employment in the informal economy in Morocco than in other MENA countries (nearly 70%, compared to 30-50% in Lebanon, Yemen, Egypt, WBGS, Algeria and Syria (OECD-WEF 2012 citing Heintz and Chang, 2007).

12. Statistically, the low rate of female labour force participation is the dominant explanatory factor in the level of entrepreneurial activity at all stages of the firm life cycle (Reynolds, P., 2013, forthcoming).

13. Nascent ventures are those start-ups that have not reported profits; new firms are considered those with up to 3 and a half years of profitable operation; this is one year longer than the infant firms in the assessment in the previous section.

14. Reynolds reports on the determinants of firm creation and found that "personal attributes, national cultural and social norms, and personal context were much more likely to be associated with individual participation in business creation than characteristics of the national economy, economic structure, population readiness for business creation or centralised control of business activity" (the indicators are listed in Table 2.3). The primary policy implication drawn from this finding is that "efforts to directly prepare individuals for business creation are more likely to have an impact compared to adjustments in regulatory procedures or legal standards (Reynolds, P., 2011, p. 316).

15. For example, different independent variables change at different speeds so some may precede and others cause variation in business creation. A second issue is the need to normalise across all 75 countries so each, therefore, is represented in terms of its relationship to the average values for all 75. Furthermore, all countries are given equal weight, regardless of substantial differences in the size of human and business populations.

16. This provides a standardised measure of variation across all factors.

17. The largest country in the sample, China, had a 2009 population of 1.3 billion that is 12 600 times larger than the smallest, Tonga, with 103 000.

18. A detailed analysis is provided in (Reynolds, P., 2013, forthcoming).

Bibliography

Acs, Z. and E. Autio (2011), *The Global Development and Entrepreneurship Index: A Brief Explanation*, Presentation, Victoria and Albert Museum, London, March.

Bosma, N. and J. Levie (2010), *Global Entrepreneurship Monitor: 2009 Global Report*, Babson College, Universidad del Desarrollo and Reykjavik University, London.

Hattab, H. (2009), *GEM Egypt Entrepreneurship Report, 2008*, GERA, London.

IDRC (2010), *GEM-MENA Regional Report 2009*, IDRC, Ottawa.

OECD (2011), *Entrepreneurship at a Glance 2011*, OECD, Paris.

OECD-World Economic Forum (2011), *Arab World Competitiveness Report 2011-2012*, World Economic Forum, Geneva.

Reynolds, P. (2013, forthcoming), *Firm Creation in the Business Life Course: MENA Countries in the Global Context*, OECD-IDRC, Paris and Ottawa.

Reynolds, P. (2011), "New Firm Creation: A Global Assessment of National, Contextual, and Individual Factors", *Foundations and Trends in Entrepreneurship*, 6 (5-6), 315-496.

Reynolds, P., N. Bosma, E. Autio, S. Hunt, N. De Bono, I. Servais, P. Lopez-Garcia and N. Chin (2005), "Global entrepreneurship monitor; Data collection design and implementation, 1998-2003", *Small Business Economics*, 24:205-231.

World Bank (2012), *World Development Indicators, 2012*, World Bank, Washington.

World Bank.(2011), *Entrepreneurship Snapshots 2010, Measuring the Impact of the Financial Crisis on New Business Registration*, IBRD/World Bank, Washington.

World Bank (2010), *The Environment for Women's Entrepreneurship in the Middle East and North Africa Region*, World Bank, Washington.

World Bank (2009), *Gender-based differences among entrepreneurs and workers in Lebanon*, World Bank, Washington. Available at: *https://openknowledge.worldbank.org/handle/10986/3164*. Last access 20 June 2012.

Chapter 3

High growth new enterprises owned by graduates

This chapter zooms in from the "big picture" presented in Chapter 2 towards a more "in-depth" analysis of a very small number of enterprises in MENA: high growth new enterprises owned by graduates. These are especially relevant for policy makers as they have the potential to contribute substantially to job and wealth creation.

To study the characteristics and challenges of these high growth enterprises, interviews were conducted with 20 entrepreneurs in five different countries (Egypt, Jordan, Morocco, Tunisia and UAE) covering a wide range of sectors. The case studies illustrate that most high growth firms have several owners, with university degrees and some, but diverse, previous work experience. Two thirds of these firms reported difficulties with access to finance, the recruitment of skilled labour, burdensome government regulation and corruption in the start-up process. Thus new business owners feel there is an opportunity for significant improvements, in particular in the area of access to finance and government regulation. While there is no overarching agreement on what governments need to do, some specific suggestions by entrepreneurs are given at the end of this chapter.

Introduction and methodology

Chapter 2 painted a "big picture" of the scale and nature of enterprising activity in MENA countries – comprising perhaps 5 million people in Egypt alone. This chapter shifts the focus radically towards a more in-depth review of a very small number of new enterprises that perhaps have the potential to go on and become significant contributors to wealth and job creation in the future.

The justification for this shift is that such enterprises are expected to have a positive and considerable direct impact on the economy by creating jobs for their employees and wealth for their owners. They may also have a secondary positive effect by generating wealth for their suppliers and their employees, and by providing valuable goods and services for their customers. Thus, even though they are small in number, they can have a considerable economic multiplier effect.

The focus will be on young firms with economic potential, defined as those starting after 2005 and established by graduates. The economic crisis that engulfed a number of MENA countries since 2008 emphasises the need for policy makers to understand the role of such firms and to give their owners' views serious consideration.

Interviews with new business owners allow an assessment of the entrepreneurial experience based on their opinions and perceptions. The common criterion for selecting the companies was their age, i.e. they had been trading for fewer than six years. This is close (although not exactly corresponding) to the definition of young enterprises used in Chapter 2, where these firms are defined as registering up to five years of profits.

Although cases were not selected because of the educational levels of their owner-managers, in practice all the case studies were of enterprises established or managed by individuals with graduate or postgraduate education. The selection process of case studies influenced this outcome in that some, though not all, of the interviews were arranged through the network of alumni and contacts of professors of the business schools and universities co-operating in the study.

Four new enterprises covering a wide range of sectors of economic activity for each of the five countries – Egypt, Jordan, Morocco, Tunisia and the UAE – took part in the study. Data were collected through face-to-face interviews with the owner of the new enterprise, but often supplemented by telephone or mail contact. The interview schedule included open and flexible questions, allowing the business owners to express their opinions and experiences. Box 3.1 provides further details about the methodology.

> ## Box 3.1. **Methodological reach and implications of the case studies**
>
> The 20 case studies used a common outline asking the same questions. The analysis is focused on details and reasons for starting the business; the scale and aspirations of growth; background information about the founders; characteristics and issues concerning access to finance; competitiveness; attitudes to enterprise in their communities; and views on how governments can stimulate entrepreneurship. The report does not disclose specific information about individual companies.
>
> Clearly, 20 firms cannot be a statistically representative sample of the gazelle population in MENA countries, but interviews with them can help to explore in greater depth issues of concern to this group of business owners. What it does not do is to imply that public policies should be based exclusively on these exceptional success stories or upon narrow definitions of high-impact enterprises (OECD, 2010). It does emphasise that despite their diversity and their different ways of expressing matters there are several issues that the owners of these businesses regard as major constraints on the growth of their business. These are access to finance, regulatory constraints and a shortage of skilled labour – although the emphasis upon these varies between countries.
>
> Despite clearly identifying these areas of concern, re-focusing public policy upon such firms presents challenges in all countries, the most notable of which is identifying high-impact enterprises.
>
> The approach and analysis of the report, however, constitutes a significant advance in the examination of gazelles in the MENA region. By looking first at the broad picture of enterprise activity in MENA and then at the 20 firms selected, the report provides a reasonably complete analysis of these enterprises and their characteristics. Based on the analysis, it also offers an initial but meaningful set of policy options open to policymakers in MENA economies, based on OECD and MENA experience.

Enterprises characteristics

The analysed businesses are new, show considerable employment growth and are highly valuable

The case-study businesses are all new and some are very new. All have been established since 2005 and half of them after 2008. They are found in a wide diversity of sectors with four businesses in manufacturing and three in restaurants and retailing. The rest cover sectors such as construction, personal and business services.

Only one was clearly high-tech. Fewer than half made no claim to be high-tech, but a sizeable number clearly embraced new technology in differing aspects of their business.

Despite their very recent establishment, the firms vary considerably in size, and some are very large. Table 3.1 shows that, although about a third of the sample have fewer than 10 employees, six firms have more than 50 employees, and the largest firm currently has 300 full time employees. For one case, we have no employment information.

Some of the businesses are highly valuable. Although a number of owners were either unable or unwilling to place a market value on their businesses, in five cases the owner

Table 3.1. **Current Employment size of surveyed firms is mostly below 50 workers**

	≤ 10 workers	10-49 workers	50-100 workers	100+ workers
Number of businesses	6	6	3	3

estimated it would exceed EUR 1 million. The most highly valued business was one estimated at EUR 14 million.

Registration duration and costs vary widely among countries

Registration with the government authorities had taken place for most of these businesses, of which only one was in the informal sector. However, registration was not consistent and was sometimes with only some agencies still underway.

Registration times varied considerably from one business to another and from one country to another. All the UAE businesses were registered within a week. In Egypt, the process was sometimes short, but in one case took 12 months. Similar, though less extreme, variations were found in both Jordan and Tunisia.

The cost of registering the business also varied considerably. In part, the variation was because some firms were seeking a Stock Exchange quotation, whereas others were only seeking the most basic form of registration. The Tunisian costs varied from EUR 25 to EUR 1 750, whereas the variation in Jordan was more modest, varying only from EUR 90 to EUR 450. However, there were suggestions that the process was subject to corruption. One respondent reported that, "legally it cost me about EGP 2 000, but more than EGP 20 000 under the table as facilitation fees".

The main motivation to start a business is the identification of a market need

Founders gave a wide variety of reasons for starting their businesses. Sole individuals owned only six businesses in the sample, while combinations of people, including, spouses, other family, friends and colleagues, owned the bulk of the rest.

For some, the reason for starting the business was the identification of a market need or niche that they felt able to fill, with that knowledge coming directly from previous work activity. This was the dominant reason, often combined with the influences discussed below. Dissatisfaction with previous work prospects was also referred to frequently. A third motivation was seeking a form of employment that provided satisfaction to the owner, especially when combined with childcare or specific family circumstances.

Box 3.2 displays this diversity of motives in direct quotations.

Box 3.2. **Motivations for starting a business**

"Having been employed to set up the business of a large UK Public Limited Corporation in the Middle East and having done so with success, a combination of events allowed the stars to align. The biggest driver was that I had identified a gap in the market, an opportunity in an emerging market but the policies, procedures, lack of cultural understanding and risk averse nature of the PLC did not allow us to take advantage. Moreover the attitude of this large PLC towards business in the region alienated local partners and started to damage long term relationships that I had. I wanted to take advantage of the opportunity, of the ability of those who I invited to join me and in the strength of my relationships. Ultimately we wanted to make a change whilst building an exciting profitable business. I believe we have done pretty well so far."

"As a graduate of fine arts I have worked on several art projects as a freelancer, at a later stage, I joined a couple of well-known publishing houses. Yet, after getting married and having kids, keeping the balance was difficult so my husband, who is also a fine arts-graduate and works as graphic designer, suggested we start our own business to make use of our expertise and thus we dedicated a space in our house to carry on our activities."

Source: Interviews (2011).

New enterprises face a broad variety of challenges including competition, access to finance, corruption and a lack of skilled labour

The problems faced by these new enterprises in their early days were diverse but access to finance, competition and problems recruiting skilled labour were widespread. Table 3.2 shows the responses given by owners to questions about the problems that they faced in their early days and those that they currently face. In some instances, since many are very new firms, the problems are the same, but in most, they are different.

This is an important table for several reasons. First, it demonstrates that all the new firms initially and at the time of the interview experienced at least one, and normally more than one of the problem areas identified in the table. Second, it demonstrates that not all businesses experience the same problems. Indeed the striking feature of the table is that almost every problem area was identified by at least one business. The only exception is that for many firms current (macro-economic) conditions were generally worse than when the business began.

Despite the range of problems reported, Table 3.2 shows that the most frequently referred to problem areas during a business start-up were access to finance, competition from rivals and an inability to obtain skilled employees. Some two thirds of firms referred to these factors.

Table 3.2. **The most common problems faced by new enterprises at start and at the time of interview ("currently") are access to finance, competition and corruption**

Problem	Faced at start	Currently faced
Economic conditions	2	4
Competition	9	7
Interest rates or access to finance	9	6
Inflation or cost of inputs	2	3
Cash-flow payments or debtors	6	5
Government regulations	6	4
Lack of skilled employees	7	3
High wage rates	2	3
Total tax burden	1	3
Lack of time/capacity	2	–
Corruption	6	5
Lack reliable basic services	2	2
Lack of internal management skills	–	2
NONE	–	–

In general, however, firms are less likely to report problems currently than during the start-up phase, which implies that the firms have addressed some of them by themselves. Amongst the top issues of current concern are competition and lack of skilled employees, although access to finance continues to be a problem for a minority of firms.

Not shown in the table are differences between countries. For example, problems over access to finance are widely referred to by the UAE and Jordanian firms, but by none of the Egyptian firms. Several Moroccan firms referred to problems with government regulations and corruption but not those in either Jordan or Tunisia.

New enterprises widen their market with time

The vast majority of the businesses start by selling locally, but then geographically widen their markets over time. Table 3.3 shows that even businesses that expect to perform well are initially heavily dependent upon the local market. Even so, for the three firms that did begin by having overseas sales immediately, export sales were a major source of revenue.

What is clear from the Table is that, with time, businesses expand the geographical range of their sales. Sales into local markets fall from 58% to 50%, whereas overseas sales rise from 18% to 21%.

Table 3.3. **New enterprises expand locally in the course of their development**

Market percentage	At start	Currently
≤ 20 miles	57.6	49.8
20-100 miles	13.8	19.3
≥ 100 miles but national	7	8.1
Overseas	17.9	21.3

Note: The results do not add up to 100%, because of incomplete answers.

These new enterprises have grown rapidly and have high aspirations for the future

The growth in employment since start-up in some of these enterprises has been remarkably high and their owners expect this to continue in the next few years. This is shown in Table 3.4, which distinguishes between firms of different sizes The first row shows employment when the businesses began. With the exception of one firm, which was a cross-border transfer, all firms specifying their employment had fewer than 50 workers when they began and 12 of them had fewer than ten. In aggregate, when they began, these firms employed 213 full- and part-time workers.[1]

The second row of the table shows the current employment, shown earlier as Table 3.1. Where it differs is by including the total number of full- and part-time employees. Comparing rows 1 and 2 of Table 3.4 it can be seen that employment has risen strikingly from 213 to 1107. This is primarily a reflection of the increase in the number of firms employing 50 or more workers, which have risen from one to six.

Table 3.4. **Employment distributions**

	≤ 10 workers	10-49 workers	50-100 workers	100+ workers	Total employment [full and part time]
At start	12	6	1	0	213
Currently	6	6	3	3	1 107
Two years from now	7	3	2	6	1 469

Note: Not all respondents provided answers to all these questions.

The third row of Table 3.4 shows the number of firms expecting to have employment in the four size categories in two years' time. It can be seen that almost one third of firms providing employment data expect to have more than 100 full time workers by 2013. If achieved, this will be a remarkable expansion, given that none of these firms will have been trading at that time for a decade. The total number of jobs is forecasted to rise to 1 469, which is a 33% increase over two years.

There is, of course, the risk of over-optimism that consistently characterises the forecasts of entrepreneurs, but the fact that there has been a sharp rise in employment since start-up does provide some confidence in the projections. It also points to the direct employment-creation role played by such enterprises.

Who are the founders of these businesses and what sort of backgrounds do they have?

All the business founders are graduates in a variety of subjects, but the majority in science or engineering, with some in arts-related subjects. A small number have business-related qualifications such as MBAs.

What is clear is that the founders are highly educated individuals, compared even with those creating new firms in developed countries. For example, a random sample of those starting new enterprises in all sectors in England and Wales found that 27% of start-ups were launched by graduates.[2]

The majority of founders are male. There are 15 males and 5 females who are the lead partner, although there is a male who is at least a part owner in an enterprise in 17 cases.

There is a wide diversity in the ages of the founder. The oldest founder was 56 years of age and the youngest was 27. The majority are currently in the 30-50 age range, which also is very similar to the findings of Greene *et al.* (2008) for England where the median age of a new firm owner was around 40.

There is also a range of prior experience of business owners. A quarter currently own another enterprise, and one works as an employee in another firm, but the remainder have no other business interests. Again, this is close to the 24% finding of Greene *et al.* for England. Individuals who had owned a business before created seven of the firms, so about two-thirds were begun by someone starting for the first time. This, again, is in line with the Greene *et al.* findings. Of those that had prior business-ownership experience, only one continues to trade in their former enterprise. The others had closed their prior firms before they began their current enterprises.

The business owners were most likely to have been born and lived in the country where they started their businesses. While only one of the four UAE founders are born there, in Egypt, Morocco and Jordan all founders were born in that country. However this diversity is also to be expected. Immigrants to countries are frequently an important source of enterprise[3] but this contribution is extremely diverse. For example the Greene *et al.* findings are that for one area of England – Teesside- two thirds of new firm founders were born in the area, whereas in another – Buckinghamshire – this was only one quarter. This emphasises that there is no clear personal background from which potentially high-performance entrepreneurs emerge.

The attitudes of business owners

All the respondents said that starting a business had been the right decision for them. Table 3.5 reports their responses to questions about themselves and their personal satisfaction with being a business owner.

The majority of business owners view themselves as transparent, in the sense that their emotions are clear to others. However, there is a significant minority for whom this is not the case, perhaps emphasising the absence of a single "personality type" entrepreneur.

This point is even clearer in the responses to the question about whether they enjoy entering uncertain situations. Only half of the respondents said that they would be comfortable with risktaking, which is somewhat surprising from a sample of new-business owners. This proportion may still be high, compared to the population overall, but it nevertheless indicates that the founders of high-potential enterprises are by no means unanimously risk-prone.

The one characteristic that characterises virtually all new business owners is the feeling that starting the business was the right thing for them to do. In spite of all the problems that they have faced, as noted in Table 3.2, starting the business has turned out to be more desirable than other career opportunities. There was only one dissenter from this view. This rhymes with research findings in other countries that point to higher levels of job satisfaction amongst business owners than amongst employees.

There is also virtual uniformity amongst owners that starting the business has enabled them to achieve other important life goals. This may be considered surprising, since business ownership is very time-consuming, but it nevertheless again points to an all-round level of life satisfaction amongst business owners.

Access to finance

Context

Table 3.2 shows that access to finance, along with competition in the marketplace, was referred to most frequently as a difficulty faced by founders.

In many respects, this is unsurprising because prior surveys by international organisations have suggested that a lower proportion of SMEs in the MENA region than in any other "comparable" area have access to loans and lines of credit.

According to Rocha et al. (2011) approximately 20% of SMEs in the MENA region have access to a loan/credit line; with only African SMEs being in this disadvantageous position. In contrast, more than 40% of Latin American and Caribbean SMEs can access funds.

Rocha et al. (2010) also show that considerably more large firms access loans and credit lines than SMEs. For example, in the MENA region, just over 40% of large firms access this form of credit. Rocha, et al. (2010) also show that, within the MENA region, there are wide variations in the relative importance or share of all loans to enterprises for SMEs. For example, in Qatar and Bahrain only a small proportion of all loans go to SMEs. This contrasts with countries such as Morocco where about one quarter of loans go to SMEs.

Amongst the five interview countries, the share of SME to total loans is it lowest in the UAE and in Egypt at around 5%. In Jordan it is 10%, in Tunisia it is 15% and it is highest in Morocco at 24%. Since the share of loans may be considered as a proxy for the ease with which SMEs can access finance it is expected that this would be least problematic in Morocco and most difficult in UAE.

Sources of funding used by new firms

The survey found a considerable diversity of sources in funding for new firms. Table 3.5 shows the sources of finance used by new enterprises both at start up and during the 12 months prior to the interviews ("last 12 months").

Several points emerge clearly from the table. First, virtually every firm used more than one source of finance at start-up: 45 for the 20 firms. Although the combination of sources does vary widely between the firms, it points to the importance of having a range of financial options available to the new firm founder.

Table 3.5. **There is a large diversity in sources of finance used to start a business and sources used in the last 12 months**

	Used to start the business	Used in the last 12 months
Personal savings/wealth	17	7
Credit card	–	1
Trade credit	6	4
Loans or gifts from friends and family	9	6
Home mortgage	3	2
Bank loan	6	9
Bank overdraft	1	2
Equity from informal sources	1	2
Equity from financial institutions	2	4
Asset-based finance	–	1
Retained earnings	–	1
NONE	–	–
TOTAL sources	45	39

Nevertheless, almost all businesses, when they begin, draw heavily upon the wealth and personal savings of the founder. Only three businesses began without using this source of funding. Starting a business of almost any size therefore requires its owner either to have resources themselves or to be able to access them – probably from family or close friends. Although that dependency does fall as the business becomes established, many enterprises continue to draw upon these sources even after having traded for some years.

At start up, funding from friends and family is the second most frequently used source of finance for these new businesses.

The third most frequently used sources are banks, in the form of loans and/or overdrafts for about one third of the sampled firms. This contribution does vary between countries – there being no examples of bank lending to the four new enterprises in Jordan, but three in Tunisia. External equity provision is rare for new enterprises, with only one firm out of 20 obtaining this from a formal source, although another firm obtained some informal [Angel] equity.

The final source used by a significant number of new firms when they began was trade credit in the form of goods or services provided prior to payment from the supplier. Six cases used this source and there was reference to it in all five countries.

The sources of finance not used in the start-up phase are also important. Formal venture capital is rare as a source of start-up funding, but so is the use of credit cards or any form of asset-based finance. Both these are important sources of finance for new firms in wealthier economies, so their absence in MENA countries perhaps points to a less diverse range of financing options open to new enterprises in this region.

The second column of the Table shows that different combinations of funding were in use at the time of the survey and that, since start-up, there is now less dependence on personal wealth/savings. In contrast, the importance of the bank-based sources has increased markedly and is by far the most frequently used current source, with nine firms identifying loans and two with overdrafts.

Furthermore, almost half the firms said banks were the single most important source of current finance. However, this is not true in all countries. In the UAE in particular, new firms appear to have more difficulty accessing bank finance than elsewhere.

Despite the increasing diversity of funding sources used as the enterprise develops it continues to be the case that credit cards, and asset-based finance sources, are rarely used. This contrasts starkly with, for example British SMEs, 54% of which had used credit cards as a source of business finance over the previous three years. Approximately one quarter of SMEs in the United Kingdom used leasing, hire purchase and other forms of asset finance.[4]

Success in obtaining finance from formal financial institutions

One widely used metric that seeks to capture the extent to which new and small firms can access finance from financial institutions is the proportion of firms that successfully apply for such funding. Amongst the survey firms, 73% of those applying for this form of finance were successful, which might be taken as implying that most firms succeed and perhaps even that the market for new firm finance is working well *for the specific type of surveyed firms.*

In the light of other survey findings, however, this might be a misleading conclusion. Five firm owners never even sought funding from banks for their business. The reasons they gave for this was, not that they never wanted finance, but, rather, that they felt there were too many problems in applying for it. Firms with such views are one element of a "discouraged-borrowers" group of SMEs. Such firms are now receiving much more attention from those studying SMEs' access to finance.[5] Two of the firms were in Jordan.

Several of the firms that applied for funding did not succeed on the first occasion and in some cases attempted several times to secure funds until they eventually succeeded. So, although there is a success rate of almost 75%, which is broadly in line with SMEs' success rates in other lower-middle income countries, this may give the impression that SMEs access to finance is easier than is in practice the case.

The inference drawn here is that there is merit in the financial institutions' emphasising the high success rate in order to encourage more applications, but the institutions themselves also need to do more to make that application process less challenging and intimidating.

One factor that normally positively influences the willingness of banks to provide funding is the presence of a coherent business plan. All firms in this survey stated they had such a plan, but it was not written in four cases, and, in three cases, it was only "informally" written. So, only in just over half the cases was there a formal written plan.

Unsurprisingly, the firms with the formal written plan were the most likely to review and update it twice a year.

Being competitive

Becoming, and staying, competitive is crucial for a new enterprise to be successful. The many dimensions of competitiveness were explored with the owners, with the results presented in Table 3.6. The owners were asked for their views on ten dimensions of competitiveness identified in the study and on the extent to which these were important for their business. The table reports on the proportion of respondents who believe the dimension was very important for their business.

The key factor that business owners believe makes their enterprise competitive is having high quality products and services. This was an important factor for 80% of the firms, while three others agreed that it was important. In contrast, the firm owners saw

Table 3.6. **What makes your enterprise competitive?**

Factors strongly influencing the competitiveness of your business	% saying very important
Lower prices than the competition	10
Having quality products and services	80
Serving those missed by others	50
Being first to market with a new product or service	50
Doing a better job in marketing and promotion	60
Having a superior location	35
Having modern attractive products	55
Having a management team with strong technical and scientific skills	65
Developing new or advanced technology	50
Developing new intellectual property	35

lower prices as much less important, only 12% of respondents thought this was very important or important.

A second dimension of competitiveness that respondents thought to be important was "having a management team with strong technical skills". This is an important finding since it implies that the technical and scientific skills that are delivered through graduate-level education are a key influence on competitiveness and hence on firm performance.

Finally, alongside low prices, two other factors are not seen as particularly important in making a new enterprise competitive. These are the importance of a superior location and the development of new intellectual property.

What seems to emerge is that low prices or fundamental novelty are viewed as less important to the competitiveness of a new enterprise than the "basics" of offering high quality goods and services delivered by a management team with strong technical and scientific skills.

Attitudes to entrepreneurship

This section captures the views of new graduate business owners about a number of aspects of entrepreneurship in their community. It is important to stress that respondents answered questions about their own community about which one assumes they had direct experience. These experiences are likely to vary between and within countries. Table 3.7 presents the data.

Table 3.7. **Business owners' attitudes to enterprise in their community**

The self-reported views of business owners about attitudes to enterprise in their own community	% strongly agreeing
The social norms and culture are highly supportive of success achieved through one's own personal efforts	30
Young people are encouraged to be independent and start their own businesses	20
State and local governments provide good support for those starting businesses	0
Bankers and other investors go out of their way to help businesses	5
Many of my friends have started new businesses	10
Many of my relatives have started new businesses	20

About one third of new business owners feel their communities are supportive of success achieved through one's own personal efforts. We take this to reflect communities in which successful entrepreneurship is held in high esteem. By implication, the reverse may reflect the so-called "tall poppy syndrome" in which those who excel are cut down to the size of the other poppies in the field. Although not shown in the Table, three of the four Jordanian respondents were positive about attitudes, whereas the views of the Egyptian and Tunisian respondents were much less positive. Indeed the Egyptian respondents reported that there was more likely to be hostility towards, rather than support for, success.

Broadly similar findings emerge when respondents were asked about whether their community encouraged new business creation amongst young people. Here 20% of respondents strongly held that view, with another 30% holding that view but less strongly. Again, the views across the countries differed somewhat with Jordanian respondents being broadly positive, but the reverse for the Egyptian and Moroccan respondents.

What unites this group of new business owners is that none is persuaded that state and local governments provide good support for those starting in business. Tunisian business owners expressed the most positive views, whereas the UAE, Egyptian and Morocco owners were almost consistently negative, and in several cases strongly negative.

A similar level of consistency appeared when business owners were asked for their views on the statement that bankers and investors went out of their way to help businesses. Only one business owner, a Tunisian, agreed with this statement, three offered no opinion and the remainder disagreed with differing levels of vehemence. However, it is worth linking this to finance where the survey found that virtually three quarters of those respondents who had applied for bank finance were ultimately successful, and that this is broadly in line with evidence from other lower-middle-income countries. This suggests there are important perception, as well as reality, issues in the relationship between small business owners and the finance community.

The final two rows of Table 3.7 report on whether new business owners said their friends and relatives had also begun new businesses. A positive response could reflect an entrepreneurial environment in which enterprise creation is the norm. The answers suggest this is not generally the case with only two respondents clearly pointing to friends' having started a business, although there were four cases where family members had started one. There were no cases in the UAE of either family or friends having created a new enterprise.

How can governments stimulate entrepreneurship?

None of the 20 new business owners in this survey strongly agreed with the statement that, "the state and local governments provided good support for those starting new businesses". This varied between countries, with Tunisian respondents having more positive views of state support than either the Egyptian or the UAE business owners.

This section develops the theme of what the government does, and what it might do, to help new enterprises. Respondents were asked whether they had ever participated in public programmes and, if so, what their views were about the impact of the programme on their business.

Eight firms said they had participated in government programmes to help new and small firms. Only in Jordan were there no respondents who had participated in such programmes. Of the participants, one reported a very negative experience, one was positive, one felt it to be useful, but too general, and one felt that the fit with their business was weak. One respondent provided the observation that, whilst their personal experience had been satisfactory, their "general view" was not positive. Box 3.3 captures these diverse views.

Box 3.3. Experience with government entrepreneurship support programmes

"Overall a good experience as we got many good consulting projects going, although we worked with a way below average consultant in one project… But overall, the money spent by the government does not equal the services received. The reason businesses don't complain is because they only contribute 10-20%."

"We found the public programme to be very informative. The training provided has helped to formalise working and labour processes and also to clarify business objectives and needs. It also helped to implement the business plan."

"It was relatively useful but very general and not specific enough. They offer only general training in entrepreneurship competences and skills."

Source: Interviews (2011).

Non-participants were asked why they had not participated in public programmes. Their responses were evenly divided between those who claimed they were unaware of the programme and those who felt the existing suite of programmes were not suitable for their business and therefore would provide it with little value.

Finally respondents were asked the more open-ended question of what they felt government could do to help their business. This generated a wide range of highly disparate, and frequently contradictory, responses. These are reported in Box 3.4.

The first two responses capture the polar opposites in approach – with one favouring minimal government and the other favouring a much more supportive but "hands-on" approach. Between those two extremes are other respondents seeking "better but not necessarily more government". These include a range of suggestions such as a simpler and swifter issuing of licenses, the establishment of an easy small-claims court to encourage fewer payment delays and facilitation of part time working.

The second issue raised was the nature and scale of the tax regime. More than half the respondents raised some aspect of the tax regime, the majority simply wanting either a general reduction in taxes or, more frequently, a reduction in, or removal of, those taxes which they felt were disproportionately paid by their enterprise.

The final set of issues that was raised is not specific to the individual business, but would help businesses generally to perform better. These issues were much less frequently raised by respondents but included matters such as the reliable provision of basic economic infrastructure and services; ensuring there is a supply of well-trained workers; reducing the power of monopolists and leading a fight against corruption.

The diverse, and even contradictory, responses which the respondents provided when asked what governments could do to help their business emphasises there is no single

---

Box 3.4. **The general role of government**

- Do nothing – keep away from my business.
- The creation of a macro-economic support policy for the sustainability of entrepreneurship and SMEs, along with a governing body to oversee the implementation of this policy.
- A simplification of regulations, such as easy and straight licenses.
- Having a quick, cheap and easy small-claims court would be of real value to overcome difficulties with cash-flow and debtor payments.
- In the UAE part-time working is effectively forbidden. This prevents new enterprises from growing because they often could not afford full-time employees. So it is important that part-time working should be allowed.

The tax regime

- The government tax regime makes us uncompetitive.
- A reduction in income tax.
- Value Added Tax is too easily avoided by competitors who are either too small to pay it or who evaded it and so were able to charge lower prices to customers hence under-cutting legitimate firms.
- The cost of property registration is prohibitively high.

Other issues

- Public services such as transport, water and electricity and broadband access is poor and almost always unreliable.
- Government should improve access to skilled workers. Businesses seeking to compete with overseas enterprises are particularly hampered.
- Government could provide real help to small firms by addressing these "macro" issues.
- Government should break up monopolies because these firms charge high prices for their products.
- Fight corruption.

"magic bullet" for governments to fire so as to satisfy even the bulk of growing SMEs. In particular there is a sharp divide between those SMEs who simply want less government, and those who want better government. There is also the difficulty that tax payments are also consistently seen by SME owners as regressive and potentially undermining of their business, yet most governments require income to provide public services.

Despite these contradictions there are also important pointers for governments wishing to improve the environment for new enterprises with growth potential. At the very practical level the provision of courts to speed payment procedures is desirable, as is attacking monopolies and the provision of economic infrastructure. In some countries the elimination of corruption is of paramount importance.

Summary and conclusions

This chapter has reported the results of interviews with the owners of 20 new enterprises in five MENA countries: Egypt, Jordan, Morocco, Tunisia and UAE. All these businesses are new – defined as established since 2005 – and every business is owned by a graduate.

Since prior research has shown a broadly positive link between the educational qualifications of the founder and the performance of the enterprise, we expect these to be high-performing, and high-potential, ventures.

This expectation is realised since, as a group, these graduate-owned new firms have grown rapidly since they were established. Furthermore, they also expect to continue to grow in the future – some even more rapidly than they have in the past.

Six of the businesses currently have more than 50 workers and five are valued at more than EUR 1 million, even though they are all less than six years old.

However this process of growth has not been easy and many problems have had to be overcome. Virtually two thirds of new firms, when they began, reported experiencing problems with access to finance and the recruitment of skilled labour. Government regulations, combined with corruption, were also frequently mentioned as problems to be addressed.

The firms have taken steps to address these problems and so they are mentioned by fewer firms. Nevertheless, access to finance continues to be a difficulty facing a number of firms, together with the recruitment of skilled labour. The competition faced by the firm in its marketplace is also another important current problem.

In spite of having all these problems, the owners of new firms believe that the creation of an enterprise has been a good career choice for them. It has also given them the opportunity to satisfy other important life-goals.

Business owners derive personal satisfaction from entrepreneurship as career choice. Even so, they feel governments can make significant improvements in policy making and in improving access to finance.

The study points to a strong, and widely-held, view that the financial sector is providing inadequate access to finance for new and small enterprises. Only one out of 20 firms agreed strongly that banks went out of their way to assist enterprises.

At face value this might imply that few of these firms received bank funding, but this is not the case. More than two thirds of those firms that applied for bank funding actually received it. The problem is that a number of enterprises never sought funding. They were "discouraged" in the sense of not applying because they thought either that they would be rejected or that the bureaucracy would be too onerous. A second group are those who, although they eventually received funding, found the process both time-consuming and problematic because of having to try a number of sources before being accepted.

There is clearly a need for a considerably better dialogue between the finance and the enterprise community so as to understand better the perspectives of the other. It emphasises that this is a marketplace where information is highly imperfect and perhaps one in which all parties could benefit from greater interaction.

Although new enterprise owners' view of government is slightly more positive than their views of the providers of finance, it is the case that there are many suggestions of how government can assist enterprises of this type.

The potentially considerable economic impact of these enterprises means that their views and suggestions need to be taken very seriously. Unfortunately, these suggestions are disparate, and sometimes inconsistent with one another. There is no overarching agreement on what government needs to do.

Even so, there are some consistent and recurring themes. These are: reducing regulations and the associated corruption; a review of the tax system: its fairness, because those who pay it are at a disadvantage compared with those who evade or avoid it; the importance of basic reliable public services such as water, electricity and transport; and the provision of a legal structure which operates speedily and at low cost.

Notes

1. There is incomplete data for one firm.

2. Greene *et al.* (2008).

3. Levy (2007) emphasises this contribution.

4. See Figure 16.2 of Storey and Greene (2010).

5. Discouraged borrowers are those who, in conditions of perfect information would have applied for loans. They comprise those who are discouraged by the application costs and those who are discouraged because they fear they will be rejected. See Kon and Storey (2003).

Bibliography

Greene, F.J., K.M. Mole and D.J. Storey (2008), "Three Decades of Enterprise Culture: Entrepreneurship", Economic Regeneration and Public Policy, Palgrave, New York.

OECD (2010), *High-Growth Enterprises: What Governments Can Do to Make a Difference*, OECD, Paris.

Rocha, R., S. Farazi, R. Khouri and D. Pearce (2010), "The Status of Bank Lending to SMEs in the Middle and North Africa Region: The Results of a Joint Survey by the Union of Arab Banks and the World Bank", The World Bank and The Union of Arab Banks, Washington, DC, and Beirut.

Rocha, R., S. Farazi, R. Khouri, and D. Pearce (2011), "The Status of Bank Lending to SMEs in the Middle East and North Africa Region", *World Bank Policy Research Working Paper*, No. 5607.

Chapter 4

The entrepreneurship and SME policy regime in five MENA countries

This chapter reviews current SME and entrepreneurship policies from OECD experience. The chapter aims at providing policy guidance for governments seeking to promote high growth enterprises.

While there is no single best practice policy or a "one size fits it all" programme, the report makes policy recommendations in the areas of regulatory reform, access to finance and the promotion of women as entrepreneurs. It concludes that careful evaluation of governments' support programmes is necessary to identify which policies work best in their specific context.

Introduction

This chapter aims to provide insights for policymakers in MENA countries seeking to enhance enterprise development and entrepreneurship. Although such policies have often been established only relatively recently in MENA economies, they have generally a longer history in OECD countries and some emerging economies. Cross-country SME and entrepreneurship policy reviews undertaken at the OECD for nearly 20 years have led to the development of a framework that could constitute the basis for establishing good practice in the area.

The first section presents a framework as a benchmark for good practice, which, although developed in high-income countries, has some valid applications in middle-income countries. The chapter then provides a review of current government policies intended to promote enterprise and entrepreneurship in Morocco, Tunisia, Egypt, Jordan and the UAE, including some updates to the comprehensive coverage provided by Stevenson (2010). The final section of the chapter sets out the key choices facing public policy makers seeking to enhance enterprise in MENA countries. It draws upon the policy frameworks in this chapter but also the key findings from Chapter 2 on enterprise creation and the case studies of graduate-owned enterprises described in Chapter 3.

The role of public policy on SME and entrepreneurship promotion

Chapter 1 demonstrated the importance of entrepreneurship and enterprise development and, in particular, the relevance of start-ups, innovative firms and high growth enterprises. What can governments do to promote enterprise creation and development, including of high-potential firms? What approaches should they take? Should they focus on a specific sector of the enterprise population, a specific industry or a territory; or should policies avoid targeting any specific type of firms and entrepreneurs? What combinations (if any) of both broad approaches should be taken?

Governments in the OECD area have long recognised the role of SME development. For instance, in 1953, the United States founded the Small Business Administration, to help small firms access finance, counselling and other forms of assistance. Along the same lines, governments in the European Union adopted a "Small Business Act for Europe", which recognises the importance of SMEs for prosperity and which puts forward ten principles to guide the conception and implementation of policies both at EU and member-state level (EC, 2008).These principles included: creating a business environment in which entrepreneurship is rewarded; ensuring that honest entrepreneurs who have faced bankruptcy quickly get a second chance; designing rules under a "Think Small First" principle which weights the burdens of new regulations in the smallest firms; promoting the upgrading of skills in SMEs and all forms of innovation; and facilitating SMEs' access to finance; amongst others.

The OECD-Eurostat Entrepreneurship Indicators Programme (EIP) distinguishes between the *manifestation* of entrepreneurship ("entrepreneurial performance"), the factors that influence it ("determinants"), and the impacts of entrepreneurship on the economy or society. Figure 4.1 presents a simplified structure of the framework.

Figure 4.1. **SME and entrepreneurship development**

The OECD-Eurostat Entrepreneurship Indicators Programme Framework

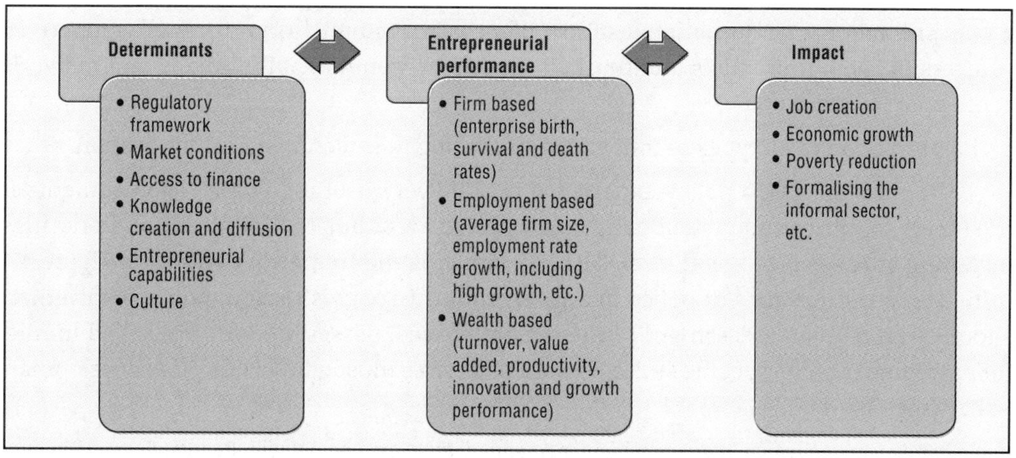

Determinants	**Entrepreneurial performance**	**Impact**
• Regulatory framework • Market conditions • Access to finance • Knowledge creation and diffusion • Entrepreneurial capabilities • Culture	• Firm based (enterprise birth, survival and death rates) • Employment based (average firm size, employment rate growth, including high growth, etc.) • Wealth based (turnover, value added, productivity, innovation and growth performance)	• Job creation • Economic growth • Poverty reduction • Formalising the informal sector, etc.

Source: Adapted from OECD (2011), *Entrepreneurship at a Glance*, OECD, Paris.

Similarly, the World Bank's *Doing Business* project and database compile and analyse regulations affecting business activity in 183 countries through different stages or areas of the business life cycle, including starting a business, getting credit, paying taxes, employing people and resolving insolvency.

Policy evidence from OECD countries on high growth enterprises

OECD (2010a) shows that high growth firms do not have a specific set of characteristics that allow their easy identification. Therefore, an appropriate policy strategy would be to create conditions for any firm to become high growth or to experience one or more episodes of high growth, rather than to select or target firms with specific characteristics, such as sector, age, past performance or the nature of the founder. In particular, policy approaches should encompass the following elements:[1]

● improving the business environment and removing disincentives to growth, such as administrative or tax obligations related to entering a large firm size class;

● raising the ambitions of new and existing business owners;

● supporting the provision of training and skills development in young and small firms, especially the technical and managerial skills necessary to cope with the pressures created by high growth;

● when necessary, improving access to debt and equity finance for new and small firms; in particular, to fund investment in research and development and the acquisition and development of intangible assets (which are essential for innovative firms whose main assets are not physical); and

● promoting innovation and internationalisation activities of new and small firms for their potential role as factors of enterprise growth.

Within this context, a survey undertaken by the OECD among members and observers to the OECD Working Party on SMEs and Entrepreneurship (WPSMEE) revealed some points of policy convergence, in particular (OECD, 2010a):

● a strong sectorial focus in some cases, with some policies targeting strategic technologies such as energy efficiency, high-technology systems, and bio technology;

- improving the business environment and cutting red tape (several countries);

- incorporating entrepreneurship into school curriculums;

- the promotion of internationalisation of new and small firms, through support for diversification of products and markets for export, commercial missions and networks of export centres; and

- the promotion of all types of innovation, including non-technological innovation.

Although the OECD policy experience may be very useful guidance, governments in the MENA countries should tailor any policy design according to their needs and priorities, including at the sub-national level. The key lesson is the framework shown in Figure 4.1, rather than the specifics of policy in a given country. For this reason, policy involvement should start with an assessment of the strengths, weaknesses, opportunities and hurdles for entrepreneurship; specific strategies and objectives must guide enterprise development policy (see Chapter 5).

The information in the following section draws on the World Bank's *Doing Business* project and from evidence at the country level. It describes the general business environment for SMEs, entrepreneurs and for general enterprise activity in the five MENA economies where business case studies were undertaken.

The policy frameworks in Egypt, Jordan, Morocco, Tunisia and the UAE

The regulatory environment is widely recognised as one of the key determinants of the scale and nature of enterprise activity in a country. Table 4.1 shows the results of the World Bank's *Doing Business* for the five MENA countries for which case studies were undertaken and focusing on the indicators that were identified as areas of concern from the case studies analysed in Chapter 3. In using the World Bank indicators, there is no implication that they capture perfectly the difficulties faced by new enterprises in the five countries, but they are a broadly helpful and easily accessible set of data from a reputable organisation.[2]

Table 4.1. **Ease of Doing Business 2012: Morocco, Tunisia, Egypt, Jordan and the UAE**

	Morocco	Tunisia	Egypt	Jordan	UAE
Ease of doing business RANK POSITION OUT OF 186	94	46	110	96	33
Starting a business RANK POSITION	07	56	01	06	10
Number of procedures NUMBER	6	10	6	7	7
Length of time in days NUMBER	12	11	7	12	13
Cost (% of income per capita) COST	15.7	4.2	5.6	13.9	5.6

Source: Ease of Doing Business Survey, World Bank, Washington, DC, 2012.

The top line of the Table shows the position in the league table of the five countries when taking account of all of the *Ease of Doing Business* measures. Recalling that 183 countries are included, the country with the most positive regulatory framework is the UAE at position 33. This emphasises that the MENA countries, overall, perform poorly on these criteria, implying that they have a regulatory environment in which it is less easy to do business than in many other countries.

There are also marked differences between the five MENA countries. The UAE and Tunisia appear to have a regulatory environment that is considerably easier than it is in both Jordan and Morocco, which, in turn, is some way ahead of Egypt. Overall, Egypt comes in at position 110.

The remaining four rows of the table provide more detail on different dimensions of the regulatory framework, most notably the ease and cost of starting a business. The second row shows that, although Egypt is in position 110 in the overall index, it appears to be relatively easy and inexpensive, by international standards, to start a business in that country.[3] This is not, however, the case for either Morocco or Jordan, where starting a business is a lengthy and costly process by international standards.

Table 4.2 seeks to develop this basic data by providing a brief country commentary on the regulatory environment that draws upon the observations of OECD country experts. The general picture that emerges fits closely with the views expressed by the graduate entrepreneurs in Chapter 3 and the World Bank data. It is that doing business is perceived to be difficult, despite the fact that several of the countries have sought to introduce regulatory improvements. The prevalent view is that there are an excessive number of

Table 4.2. **Regulatory framework: Country commentary**

	Commentary
Morocco	Morocco's position in the World Bank Survey has slipped somewhat in recent years from Rank 59 to its current position of 94, in spite of several government initiatives to promote enterprise and the desire and enthusiasm of many individuals. New business creation rates are low and have not increased recently. The evidence from respondents is that administrative procedures in Morocco hinder business creation and development. They also emphasised that the regulatory environment is very challenging because of the corrupt enforcement of regulations. The OECD analysed the regulatory environment in Morocco in its *Business Climate Development Strategy* (OECD, 2011). It concluded that the measures taken so far targeted administrative simplification and regulation. However, they fell short of profound reform and effective implementation. Moreover, they did not address reform requirements in the area of labour policies, social security contributions, contract enforcement, income tax, and issuing construction permits.[1]
Tunisia	Tunisia's position at 46 is good by MENA standards and probably reflects policy changes, such as Law 72 which has favoured the emergence of an offshore industry involved in exporting, but divorced from local networks. Tunisia has a range of investment incentives designed to unify the existing investment legal framework, and to stimulate investment in export-oriented and high-tech activities.
Egypt	Events in 2011 are likely to be part of the explanation of why Egypt has slipped to overall position 110 in the 2012 *Ease of doing Business* survey, after showing continuous improvement in recent years. The key strengths of the Egyptian regulatory framework are the ease of starting a business and in trading across borders, and it has lowered the capital requirement for LLCs from EGP 50 000 to EGP 2 000. However, Egypt performs poorly on the ease of closing a business, enforcing contracts, dealing with taxes and in issuing construction permits. Bankruptcy remains a crime in Egypt and this may also reduce the willingness of individuals to start an enterprise. In 2010, the OECD conducted a Business Climate Development Review (OECD, 2010) for Egypt and analysed business regulations in detail. The review suggests that the business climate still faces slow approval procedures and difficulties in registration due to uninformed civil servants.[2]
Jordan	In 2012 Jordan was in position 96 in the World Bank survey. However, it has also introduced business-friendly legislation: reducing the minimum capital for business establishment, of transfer fees for property registration, etc. Other relevant legislation includes Ministry of Industry and Trade Law 18/1998; Chamber of Industry Law 10/2005; Jordan Investment Board Law 18/1991; Investment Law 68/2003; Jordan Enterprise Development Corporation Law 33/2008; Development and Employment Fund Law 33/1992. To address information problems the Ministry of Industry and Trade created a one-stop shop in 2002; the Jordan Investment Board established its one-stop shop in May 2004. A private credit bureau has been established as well as lowering the threshold for loans to be reported to the public credit registry.
UAE	UAE has made considerable progress over time in improving its regulatory environment as captured by the World Bank *Ease of Doing Business* survey. The current rank is in position 33 overall, having started in position 118 in 2000. Among the reasons for this current high rank by MENA standards, and the improvement over time, is the tax-free environment, though many services are fee-paying. Removing the federal minimum capital requirement and streamlining procedures in construction and trading have cut red tape and enhanced e-government. The weakness of the UAE, relates to the legal environment, most notably in the area of contract enforcement. As in Egypt, bankruptcy remains a crime, possibly providing a deterrent to business creation. The UAE is also distinct in one other respect. It is that 85% of the UAE population are non-nationals on resident/work visas.

1. More detailed information, including policy recommendations, can be found in OECD (2011), *Stratégie de développement du climat des affaires*.
2. For more information, see OECD (2010), *Business Climate Development Strategy Egypt*.

regulations and that in some cases they are corruptly enforced, leading to business owners' either seeking to avoid them or to trade at or beyond the margins of legality.

The UAE could serve as a role model for R&D and technology

Capturing the extent to which countries vary in their use of modern technologies, particularly for small enterprises, is very difficult. It is even more difficult when there is a need to compare countries with widely varying income levels, since modern technologies tend to be considerably more widespread in higher-income countries.

However, two indices covering different dimensions of innovation have been developed in recent years. The first is the Global Innovation Index (GII) covering 125 countries. It produces a country composite rank position based upon five indicators of the inputs to innovation and two measures of innovation output.

A second index with a number of desirable qualities is the ICT Development Index (IDI), made up of 11 indicators covering ICT access, use and skills. It covers 159 countries of varying income levels and, because much of the data reflect individual usage of IT services, it may be more reflective of smaller enterprises than data on larger firms.

Table 4.3 presents some of the findings from both the GII and the IDI. The first column shows the position of the five MENA countries using the GII index. The remaining three columns use the IDI index. The second column in the table shows the rank position of the five MENA countries using all 11 indicators of ICT access. The final two columns present raw data for two indicators that reflect most closely technology access for small enterprises.

Table 4.3. **ICT indicators**

	Overall world position out of 125 countries Global Innovation Index	Overall world position out of 159 countries ICT Development Index	Fixed broadband Internet users per 1 000 inhabitants	Mobile cellular suscriptions per 100 inhabitants
Morocco	94	97	1.5	72.2
Tunisia	66	85	2.2	84.6
Egypt	87	96	0.9	50.6
Jordan	41	74	2.2	86.6
UAE	34	29	12.4	208.6

Sources: Global Innovation Index rankings (2011), INSEAD, Paris, Measuring the Information Society (2010), International Communication Union, Geneva.

The evidence from the table makes it clear that both the GII and the ICT indicators place the UAE significantly ahead of the other four countries, both in terms of its position overall and in terms of fixed broadband users and mobile cellular subscriptions. The data are for 2008 and matters do change quickly in this field, but it is unlikely that the relative positions of the countries will have changed much in four years. Where the GII and ICT measures do differ somewhat is that Jordan performs considerably better under the GII measure, coming only seven places behind the UAE, than it does on the ICT measures.

Table 4.4 provides a brief commentary on R&D activity in each of the five countries – focusing specifically on small enterprises.

SMEs and entrepreneurs are at a comparative disadvantage in raising finance

SMEs are at a comparative disadvantage in raising finance, compared with larger enterprises. A broad rule of thumb is that the smaller and the newer the firm, the harder it is to persuade institutions to provide finance. The problem is that the financial institutions know that new, small firms are likely to be more risky, with a lower probability of repayment, than their larger, more established counterparts.

Table 4.4. **Research and development and technology: Country commentary**

	Commentary
Morocco	Investment in R&D would promote competitiveness and economic growth. The *OECD Business Climate Development Report for Morocco*[1] (OECD, 2011) observes that SMEs are not very competitive or innovative, especially in the export sector. Low value-added manufactured products still contribute disproportionately to Moroccan exports. Sectorial development plans lack innovation components. Though R&D and university research projects exist, their implementation remains weak and there are only a few R&D links between local SMEs and foreign investors. There are only a small number of incubators or support programmes for innovative enterprises. Job opportunities for research students and young graduates are limited. Morocco has also established an innovation strategy aimed at supporting a number of activities linked to industrial modernisation and privatisation, investment promotion and SME development. The strategy is based on successful projects and international experiences.
Tunisia	Tunisia has several well-established public support structures for SMEs that cover a wide range of economic sectors (Agency for the Promotion of Industry, Sectorial Technical Centres, the National Institute of Standards and Industrial Property, the Foreign Investment Agency, Development Agencies, etc.) Business Centres began in 2005. Their role was to facilitate the implementation of SME projects and provide basic services to developers and investors to launch and promote their projects. These one-stop shops provide all the administrative and legal requirements to speed the creation of a new business. Business incubators provide premises, as well as information, training and coaching, for novice entrepreneurs. *Wednesday creation* is part of the National Campaign for the Creation and Development of SMEs. It is a practical training programme for university students offered on Wednesdays covering the development of business plans and guidance with spinoffs and venture capital. Since 2005, the National Programme for Quality has offered SMEs the opportunity to apply for internationally recognised certification by providing technical assistance from local and international experts.
Egypt	Overall R&D expenditure in Egypt is very low (less than 0.5% of GDP) and private R&D expenditure is negligible. The most notable exception is large-scale R&D infrastructure projects in ICT such as Smart Village, R&D Centres of Excellence, etc. However, Egyptian firms do benefit from broadband Internet access, which was introduced in 2000. Currently 200 providers exist, making Internet access in Egypt one of the cheapest in Africa. Despite this, Internet penetration remains low ($\leq 30\%$). A complicated patent system interferes with R&D. The typical time taken from filing an application to the grant of a patent is about three years The Egyptian Organization for Standards and Quality (EOS) sets product standards. In co-operation with the Industrial Modernization Centre (IMC), EOS is undertaking a project to harmonise standards with international norms.
Jordan	Overall R&D expenditure in Jordan is amongst the highest in the Arab region at 0.32% of GDP. However, high-tech exports represent only 1% of manufactured exports and, in 2010, there were only 2 Internet broadband connections per 100 inhabitants. The Jordan Enterprise Development Corporation (JEDCO) has launched "Support to Research & Technological Development & Innovation Initiatives and Strategies in Jordan", a programme funded by the European Union with EUR 4 million to help the innovation and R&D sectors of the Jordanian economy. The project aims at increasing innovation capacity by promoting research in the private sector and by accelerating Jordan's integration into the European Research Area. The project currently provides 30 grants for start-ups of EUR 143 113 each. In addition, JEDCO founded eight incubators with 58 projects. They are distributed across the country and each focus on specific competences such as ICT, small scale manufacturing or engineering.
UAE	The UAE performs best of the five countries in the ICT and GII indices. It is a global leader in ports, trading, tourism, Islamic finance, domestic construction and has recently begun to encourage investments in free zones for technology in media, Internet, biotech, etc. The advantages the UAE possesses are its relatively high Internet and broadband penetration, having best-practice product standards and a multicultural environment. The challenges faced by the UAE are that it emphasises rote, rather than creative, learning throughout its education system and it could do more to strengthen the university-industry interface and technical co-operation among firms.

1. Available in French only: « Stratégie de Développement du Climat des Affaires » (OECD, 2011).

Of course, not all new, small firms will default, and some may go on to be highly successful, but the financial institutions do not know initially which is which. This imperfect information is characteristic of an opaque marketplace.

The key findings of a World Bank report (2011) on SME financing in MENA countries recognise these factors:

"*MENA banks quote the lack of SME transparency and the weak financial infrastructure (weak credit information, weak creditor rights and collateral infrastructure), as the main obstacles for further engagement in SME finance. Banks complain less about regulatory obstacles (e.g. interest rate ceilings), excessive competition in the SME market, or lack of demand for loans from SMEs. Within an overall environment of weak financial infrastructure, the countries that are able to strengthen creditor rights and provide more information to creditors succeed in inducing more SME lending overall or more long-term lending to SMEs.*"

Table 4.5 reflects these issues. The first two rows show that, by world standards, obtaining credit in MENA countries is very difficult. It is particularly difficult in Jordan, but even in Egypt and the UAE access is more difficult than in 78 other countries.

Table 4.5. **Access to finance**

	Morocco	Tunisia	Egypt	Jordan	UAE
Getting credit RANK POSITION	98=	98=	78=	150	78=
Enforcing contracts RANK POSITION	89	76	147	130	134
Ratio of SME loans to TOTAL loans	24%	15%	5%	10%	4%

Sources: Global Competitiveness Index 2011, taken from Rocha et al., 2010.

In part, this also reflects the difficulties of enforcing contracts- shown in row 2 of the table; the five MENA countries again perform poorly by international standards. Morocco and Tunisia do somewhat better than the other three countries.

The final row takes the findings of a World Bank survey of SME lending in MENA countries and shows that the proportion of total loans going to SMEs varies markedly between the five countries. It is highest by a considerable margin in Morocco and lowest in the UAE.

Table 4.6 develops this statistical material by providing some commentary on each of the five MENA countries. It consistently points to SMEs' reporting problems in accessing finance from formal institutions, but it also emphasise that access to finance is closely linked with issues such as the regulatory framework, most notably contract compliance.

Table 4.6. **Access to finance: Country commentary**

	Commentary
Morocco	Despite a high proportion of bank loans to SMEs, financing is one of the major barriers to company creation because of difficulties over both access and cost. This constraint reflects the graduate entrepreneurs' sources of funding, all of whom used primarily money from informal resources such as loans from family, help from parents, or own financing, as noted in Chapter 3. Access to formal financing instruments was the exception. Large companies continue to dominate the Casablanca Stock Exchange, and banks favour them over start-ups. The complicated procedures required to get loans also discourage start-up firms from seeking bank finance.
Tunisia	Banks constitute the most frequently used sources of funding for SMEs. Even so, there are difficulties in accessing bank loans and the relationship of SMEs with banks remains fragile. Guarantees are the rule for any credit application and alternative funding channels are not very visible to SMEs. This informational opacity may explain the low penetration of financial instruments for SMEs, thus self-financing and informal financing, especially profit reinvestment, remains the main source of funding for Tunisian small businesses. Funding through investment companies to venture capital (SICAR) and other nonbank financial institutions plays a minor role, whilst venture capital is not on the radar of the vast majority of SME entrepreneurs seeking finance.
Egypt	In 2009, overall domestic credit provided for the private sector was 36.2% of GDP, which was above the MENA average. The microfinance market is comparatively well-developed. At the other end of the spectrum, large firms have access to a reasonably developed credit market, with half of total bank loans going to 0.2% of (large) clients. Several new regulations have been implemented to address the gap that exists for SME funding. In 2009, a new regulation exempting Egyptian banks from the reserve requirement (14%) for loans to SMEs became effective. In 2010, 5 commercial banks (both public and private) established SME units. The SME exchange (NILEX) opened in 2007 and it now lists 70 SMEs. However, equity finance and leasing mechanisms remain underdeveloped.
Jordan	The Global Competitiveness Index ranks Jordan 150th in access to credit. This low score reflects problems in the banking sector, such as a lack of SME transparency, poor credit information from credit registries and bureaux, and weak creditor rights. Bank lending to SMEs is 10% of total loans. Taking into account that SMEs constitute more than 95% of the Jordanian Economy, this lending ratio is very low and the World Bank recommends increasing it to 25% (World Bank, 2011). To deal with this problem, the government of Jordan has begun to promote different projects that aim at increasing access to finance, such as the Tatweer project and the USAID Jordan Economic Development Programme. Moreover, Jordan supports SMEs through its Jordan Enterprise Development Corporation, which has established two venture capital funds.
UAE	The World Bank survey data shows that the UAE had the lowest proportion of SME to total loans of the five MENA countries in the sample (Rocha *et al.*, 2011). However, the role of venture capital is much more developed than in the four other countries. For example, the Abu Dhabi-based Khalifa Fund has recently expanded with USD 540 million for SME development. There are now programmes through the Mohamed bin Rashid Establishment for SMEs in Dubai, which channel venture capital and private equity *via* private firms, *e.g.* Abraaj (and Riyada with OPIC loan), Legatum. In addition, informal angel investing takes place through wealthy individuals, friends and family and there is a growing stock market, although currently volumes are thin. Access to finance is also linked to the regulatory regime. Bankruptcy is a crime that can lead to sentences in debtors' prisons. This constitutes a serious discouragement to an expatriate population who are the most likely to start an enterprise.

A second key result is that, with the exception of the UAE, there is almost no role whatever played by the formal venture-capital sector. In contrast, the role of family lending is important in all countries.

Careful evaluation is necessary to ensure effectiveness

According to the OECD, "evaluation refers to a process that seeks to determine as systematically and objectively as possible the relevance, efficiency and effect of an activity in terms of its objectives, including the analysis, implementation and administrative management of such activity" (OECD, 2008).

This definition emphasises that evaluation has an integral role to play in the policy *process*. Evaluation cannot be left "at the end of the line" to be undertaken once policy has been in operation for many years. To do so would be to consign it to the role of economic history. Instead, it has to be a key element of initial policy formulation.

This policy formulation process is set out in the COTE Framework (OECD, 2007). COTE emphasises that policy has to be Coherent and have Objectives and Targets followed by Evaluation that feeds into the policy-making process. This procedure underlies all successful policy. It also means that all organisations and individuals responsible for policy delivery have to be aware that evaluation is to take place. Once the evaluation has been undertaken, and sometimes as it is taking place, it forms the basis for dialogue with policy makers, with the objective of delivering better outcomes. The result of the evaluation can then become an input into a debate on the appropriate ways for governments and SMEs to interact.

There are several reasons for undertaking evaluations. The most important is that administering and delivering SME and entrepreneurship policy demands substantial sums of taxpayers' money.[4] Governments have a responsibility to the taxpayer to demonstrate that funds are spent in a manner likely to achieve the aims of the policy. Public auditors whose task is to ensure that expenditure is incurred where the legislators intended normally play part of this role.

Evaluators play a very different role. Their task is to assess whether the taxpayer obtained value for money from the policy. In short, did the policy work and what lessons can be learnt for improvement? Evaluations are most effective when their results enter the public domain. This emphasises not only the importance of undertaking evaluations, but also that their findings are disseminated. Evaluation, therefore, provides the informed basis for debate on policy impact.

Evaluation uses a number of criteria,[5] but at its core is the concept of additionality. This is the true impact of the scheme/programme. Whilst it is not always easy to quantify, it is likely to appear in additional output, employment, sales or export activity that can be attributed to the existence of the programme alone. In other words, activity that would not have taken place without the programme, and is attributable to the firm's participation in it.

Figure 4.2, taken from Oldsmanand Hallberg (2002), shows, for any given outcome, that policy impact can be considered as the difference between the observed outcome with the intervention, and what would have happened without it. The figure shows these two outcomes diverging after the implementation of the policy.

Although this is, in principle, a simple concept, identification of the programme's impact "*as systematically and objectively as possible*" can be challenging. There are a number of reasons for this. The first is that it is not always clear what changes might have occurred

Figure 4.2. **The impact of an intervention**

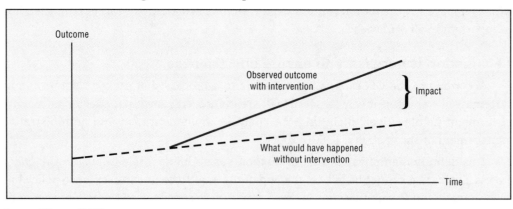

Source: Oldsman (2002).

in the firms because of participation; in other words, the outcome measures are unclear. Policy makers expect some programmes to lead to a greater likelihood of firm formation or survival, others to growth in sales, profits or employment, others to a greater likelihood of innovating or selling into overseas markets. Other programmes might be expected to enhance all these characteristics while, in other cases, it is unclear what firm characteristics are expected to show improvement. Evaluation therefore requires a decision on appropriate outcome measures.

A second problem is that participation in the programme may precede any improvement in firm growth. Using the example of Figure 4.2, the point at which the lines diverge will not necessarily be immediately after delivery of the programme. Some programmes will have their impact possibly years before others. For example, a programme in which SMEs are subsidised to participate in an international trade fair to encourage them to internationalise might have an impact upon sales within months. In contrast, a programme to fund R&D in SMEs could have little impact for several years. A programme to develop enterprise education might have no impact even for two decades because its teenaged recipients may take more than 20 years before they start a business

A third problem is the myriad of influences upon the performance of an SME, other than that of programme participation. These include the skill of the owner, the sector and location of the business, macro-economic conditions and the role of chance. In principle, only when account is fully taken of these "exogenous" factors can the impact of the programme be estimated.

The above emphasises that evaluation is not easy and often produces findings that are uncomfortable for organisations within government that are responsible for policy initiatives. Nevertheless, evaluation lies at the heart of effective policy delivery, acting in the interests of the taxpayer to ensure the implementation of public policies in a way that ensures they deliver the benefits intended in a cost-effective manner.

Policy implications

The final section of this chapter examines three, key policy choices faced by those responsible for formulating entrepreneurship and SME policy. It articulates those choices and demonstrates that the actual choices made by policy makers often differ radically, even within OECD countries.

The three key policy choices are in:

- entrepreneurship and SME policy;
- macro and micro approaches; and
- direct assistance or lowering the "burdens".

Entrepreneurship and SME policy

The first choice is over the role of entrepreneurship, as opposed to SME, policy. The distinction between them is that SME policy provides support for existing (small and medium-sized) enterprises that, by definition, are already established. This support is designed to make SMEs more competitive and so improve their likelihood of survival and growth. This support could be "hard" financial assistance in the form of grants, loans or tax reliefs or "soft" support in the form of information, training and/or advice.

In contrast, entrepreneurship policy seeks to raise the creation rate of new enterprises. For example, enterprise education to raise awareness amongst young people of the option of creating a business is an example of entrepreneurship policy, since it seeks to raise the creation rate of new firms at some point in the future.

In principle, the measures used to determine the success of such policies are simple: the extent to which there is an increase in the number of new firms attributable to the policy measures entrepreneurship policy impact. The extent to which the growth of existing firms is enhanced, leading to an improved performance of the overall economy in terms of job creation, unemployment reduction, productivity or wealth creation measures SME policy impact.

Unfortunately, although the concepts are simple, assessments of policy impact in practice need extreme care. Policy makers are faced with a critical question: given a fixed budget, how much should be spent on encouraging the creation of new firms [entrepreneurship policy], compared with providing funds to enhance the growth of existing firms [SME policy].

To assist policy makers in these key decisions, Box 4.1 explains the advantages and disadvantages of pursuing entrepreneurship policy.

Box 4.2 sets out the arguments against entrepreneurship policies.

The alternative approach – SME Policy – is one based on providing support for existing or established small businesses. One distinctive element of SME policy focuses upon enterprises with the potential to grow extremely fast and generate considerable of numbers of jobs. Box 4.3 makes the case for this approach.

Box 4.4 gives the case against selective SME policy.

The arguments presented in the Boxes should be the basis of an informed political debate. In OECD countries, the precise balance or combination of SME and entrepreneurship policy reflects both the economic and political circumstances of that country and how it wishes to develop. This emphasises that there is not a single, ideal combination.

However, it appears that the bulk of public funding in OECD countries is focused upon SME, rather than on entrepreneurship policies. Lundstom et al. (2012) found that in Sweden SME policy expenditure was up to eight times that of entrepreneurship policy. This might be taken to imply that policy makers in OECD countries believe that funding the better

---

Box 4.1. **The case for entrepreneurship policy**

Specific and individual jobs are not permanent and enduring features in modern market economies. More accurately, jobs are the concrete manifestation of a churning pool of opportunities for employment; any contribution to this pool will offset job losses, whatever the causes.

Higher levels of firm (and job) churning is associated with subsequent increases in net job growth and productivity increases. There are, of course, social costs associated with this churning. As firms and jobs are created and disappear, assets are redeployed from one business entity to another and individuals must change jobs, which is disruptive for them and their families. This, however, seems to be a fundamental feature of adaptation and change in market economies

There are two types of growth firms. Those that attract the most attention are associated with the development of entire new markets, or industries, that contribute to economic expansion. These have recently been prominent in the world of information and communication technology (ICT), with the creation of new industries. Similar patterns emerged in the development of other sectors, such as automobiles and medical technology. In these cases, there is an argument that a net gain has occurred, with a net increase in the job pool and economic value added.

When high growth firms occur in traditional, well-established sectors, the basis for growth may be more diverse. Alongside superior productivity or products, such growth may also occur through acquisition of competitors and, if the overall market (or industry) is relatively stable, certain competitors may disappear altogether. The national expansion of efficient retail firms (such as Wal-Mart or Carrefour) displaces small-scale retail firms. The benefits are lower prices and greater choice for consumers, but with a redeployment of jobs from independent retail firms to these international chains.

Finally, the sheer scale of the numbers of individuals engaged in the churning pool of employment opportunities points to its potential economic and employment significance. Box 9a illustrates this, showing the number of individuals involved in business creation in the MENA case study countries.

	Nascent entrepreneurs	Baby business owner-managers
Egypt	3 372 889	1 496 645
Jordan	253 576	191 916
Morocco	1 117 332	1 523 067
Tunisia	149 848	488 697
UAE	169 794	213 980

performance of existing firms is likely to have a bigger economic and employment impact than funding the creation of more new firms. An alternative explanation is that, because expenditure in these areas is so opaque, the information has never been available to make an explicit comparison. A third explanation is that there are also political factors at work and that the business lobby is more effective than individuals trying to start a business.

Box 4.2. **The case against entrepreneurship policy**

The first argument against promoting general firm creation is that it is a waste of resources on three grounds. The first is that the vast majority of the potential beneficiaries of such policies will never even consider starting a firm. Second, only a fraction of those who take some steps towards business creation ever "convert" in the sense of starting a business. For both these groups, therefore, there is no economic return whatsoever. The third ground is that, even if they do start, the economic significance of most new enterprises is minimal since perhaps only a third survives after six years and less than 1% of new firms have more than 20 employees after five years.

The second argument is that the link between general firm-creation rates and economic development remains unproven. It is unquestionably the case that business creation rates fall as economic development increases in low-income countries. More questionable is whether higher rates of enterprise creation in middle- and higher-income countries are either associated with, or lead to, increased wealth.

Thirdly, promoting general enterprise creation encourages optimistic but poorly resourced individuals to take a risk and, in many cases, to make their own position worse than it would have been if they had remained in either employment or unemployed. They may end up with substantial debts they are either unable to pay off, or where the payment imposes crippling financial pain on the individual.

Box 4.3. **The case for selective SME policy**

The case for providing support for existing enterprises is that all such firms have current economic significance – they employ workers, provide goods and services and contribute to the economy. Policy impact, if there is any, is therefore likely to be direct and immediate.

The case for supporting only a small proportion of (existing) firms is twofold. The first is that the large number of (small) firms in any economy means that demand for (publicly funded) support is likely to exceed supply considerably. The second is that, to be effective, the support needs to be on a scale that observably influences firm growth. This further reduces the number of firms that can be supported and implies some form of selection or rationing that should focus on SMEs with growth potential.

The justification for this is the key research finding that fast-growing firms have a direct and disproportionate impact on employment and competitiveness, with some 50% of the new jobs created by start-ups coming from only 4% of the firms. These firms transform an economy by changing the economic and competitive landscape and should be the focus of public-sector attention.

The effectiveness of the selective approach is illustrated by the success of long-established, government-funded selective technology projects, like SBIR in the United States, which can demonstrate policy impact. Elsewhere, initiatives such as the selective UK business support programmes and Business Links in Denmark), have been successful, while, in New Zealand, programmes, such as Growth Services Range, enhanced the sales, but not the value added, of participant firms.

> ### Box 4.4. **The case against selective SME policy**
>
> The central operational argument against a selective SME policy with a focus on fast-growth or high-potential firms is that it is very difficult to implement. Selecting the firms to support incurs a very high risk of choosing the wrong ones, such as those that either close or fail to grow. This is illustrated by the operations of the private venture capital sector, which, despite all the due diligence it undertakes, gets most of its investments "wrong" in the sense that they fail to obtain the return expected when the investment was initially made. This is most clearly the case with "early stage" investments of the type that might be the focus of public policy.
>
> Where venture capital makes its return is from the relatively small number of extremely successful investments but, although this is acceptable to the private sector, there are often political reservations about governments risking public money in what many might see as a gamble.
>
> A second, perhaps more fundamental, objection to selective SME policy support is that governments generally have a poor record in selecting "winners". The first criticism is that governments choose enterprises to support based on political influence, rather than expected economic performance. The second is that only the enterprises with poor economic prospects seek public support; the others obtain it from private sources.
>
> Linked to this poor record of accomplishment of governments is a third operational issue. It is that selecting the businesses to support is very difficult and requires considerable expertise and skill to be effective. Operational experience in the private sector is the most likely means of acquiring such skills. Implementing a selective policy, therefore, requires the recruitment of skilled personnel from the private sector who expect to receive salary and performance bonus packages that exceed those paid even to top government officials. A failure to attract such individuals however means the selection of investments and the provision of support to those investments risks being less professional and likely to generate a lower return.
>
> In addition to these operational problems, there remains the underlying issue of whether a focus on high growth firms is likely to be effective as a strategy for long-term wealth creation. The case favouring entrepreneurship policy notes that, whilst the growth of some fast-growth firms was also associated with overall growth in employment in their sector or the economy as a whole, this was not always the case. The growth of some retail chains has clearly led to declining employment in many smaller outlets. This view implies that, at best, selective policies can only be justified where they are restricted to certain sectors.

Micro and macro approaches

A second key policy choice facing governments wishing to promote and support new and small enterprises is the extent to which they use micro or macro approaches. The former are defined as those that focus policy explicitly on (groups) of enterprises or (groups of) individuals. These, for example, might be an existing or aspirant business owner having difficulty accessing finance because they lack access to collateral. Here an example of a micro policy would be the presence of a loan guarantee programme.

Macro policy would aim to reduce information imperfections in the market for finance and by ensuring that this marketplace was fully competitive. This might include policies to encourage the entry of new banks, the elimination of low-risk but high-return options for financial institutions, ensuring that banking arrangements with customers are fully transparent, and conducting regular reviews of competition in the SME finance marketplace. In short, macro policy does not explicitly address the problem but rather its overall context.

Box 4.5 presents several further examples of Macro policies that, although they often do not have SMEs or new enterprises as their prime targets, nevertheless frequently have a powerful influence on the creation, survival and growth of new and small enterprises.

Box 4.5. **Key macro influences**

Immigration: Immigration and return migration can powerfully influence both the nature and scale of new firm creation in a country. For example, McCormick and Wahba (2001) examined Egyptian returning migrants and found that, amongst literate individuals, overseas savings and the duration of their stay overseas increased their likelihood of being a business owner upon return. However, this was much less clearly the case for those who were not literate. Policies to enable immigrants to enter and by policies that enable migrants to return can, therefore, enhance business creation rates. The entrepreneurial impact of inward migrants is most clearly illustrated by Saxenian (2000) who found that individuals born in China started 37 public technology companies in California's Silicon Valley and people born in India started 22 others. These companies over time provided employment for more than 10 000 individuals.

Unemployment and Macro-Economic Conditions: Governments need to provide benevolent economic conditions to enable enterprises of all sizes to prosper. These conditions are low rates of inflation, buoyant aggregate demand and low unemployment. In general these conditions are helpful to small as well as to larger enterprises but, if the objective is to raise rates of new firm formation, there is evidence in several developed countries that this may be stimulated by deteriorating, rather than improving, macro-economic conditions. Some support for this comes from an examination of Egypt by Gadallah (undated) that showed that increases in unemployment were associated with increased rates of self-employment three years later.

When asked about what governments could do to help their business, a number of enterprises referred to a range of macroeconomic factors (see Chapter 3). These included the provision of reliable service infrastructure such as gas, water, electricity and a fast broadband network. They also referred to lowering levels of crime. A third generic area of significant importance to them was the level of skills of the workforce. All of these components are part of the macro-economic responsibility of government, but ones that directly enhance enterprise and entrepreneurship in an economy.

Many of the new firms surveyed in Chapter 3 were also clear that the taxation regime inhibited their willingness to develop their enterprise. This is because it adds to their cost base, it may reduce their motivation and it gives the impression of penalising those that comply. For these reasons, many countries provide considerable tax relief to small enterprises. For example, Lundstrom *et al.* (2011) report that in the United Kingdom this exceeded GBP 2 billion. However, evidence on the impact of the tax regime upon enterprise and entrepreneurship is contradictory. Some assert that a high tax regime constitutes an incentive to transfer from employment to business since the income generated is less transparent, is generally paid sometime in arrears and often has valuable allowances, none of which is available to the employee. Others assert the contrary, pointing to the disincentive effects of taxes on individual effort, Gentry and Hubbard (2000).

The above examples illustrate that a range of government policies that are often thought to be only marginally linked to issues of enterprise and entrepreneurship can, in practice, have a considerable impact upon firm creation and small-firm growth. The challenge for governments seeking to enhance enterprise is to examine macro policies and to use them positively as an alternative to, or in combination with the types of traditional policies discussed earlier this chapter.

Direct assistance or lowering the "burdens"

A third key policy choice is the extent to which governments emphasise policies that focus upon providing direct assistance, compared with those that focus upon seeking to lower the "burdens" or impediments to business creation or small firm expansion. Dennis (2005) shows this choice as a 2 × 2 matrix that makes a distinction between the provision of assistance and the lowering of impediments. This appears as Table 4.7.

Table 4.7. **A typology of public policy toward small business**

	LIMITING [MENA countries]	COMPETING [USA]
Low direct assistance		
High direct assistance	COMPENSATING [EU]	NURTURING [US minority]
	High impediments	**Low impediments**

Source: Dennis (2005).

It shows that policy makers have four options. EU countries generally choose to be in the lower right hand box which Dennis calls "compensating". This is because EU countries have relatively high by the standards of developed countries what Dennis calls "impediments" to starting and operating a business. These are quantified in the World Bank *Ease of Doing Business* survey" and reported earlier in this chapter and relate to, for example, the time and cost of registering a new enterprise. It may also reflect the implicit decision in the EU to place relatively more emphasis on SME, rather than entrepreneurship policy.

The United States has adopted a very different approach. Direct assistance from government to establish an enterprise is thought to be low, but so also are the barriers to starting a business. Competition enhancement is the focus of US small-business policy, hence it appears in a box labelled "competing" in the upper right square of Table 4.7. This suggests that the United States places more emphasis than the EU on entrepreneurship than on SME policy.

There are exceptions to this general US position. For example, the SBIR programme is probably the largest and longest-running (small) business support programme in history with an annual budget in excess of USD 2 billion. There are also large-scale programmes to promote enterprise among minorities. Taking account of these programmes, the United States can be seen through a different prism where the barriers are low but where there is also a high level of direct assistance provided. The box labelled "nurturing" recognises this duality. Other developed countries that exercise this policy choice are Canada and New Zealand. They would also appear in the lower right box.

MENA countries do not fit into any of these three boxes since, by the international standards of the World Bank *Ease of Doing Business* survey, it is both time-consuming and costly to start and operate a business. Unfortunately, there are not the compensations provided in EU countries of public funds to help competitiveness. Dennis refers to countries in this group as "limiting". They appear in the top left box.

Notes

1. Adapted from OECD (2010a).

2. The central limitation for our purpose is that the data refer to businesses that are larger than those covered here. For example, it is based on the assumption that the enterprise is a limited liability company that operates in the economy's largest business city and has start-up capital of 10 times income per capita in that country at the end of 2009. Most significantly for our purposes the firm has to have at least 10 and up to 50 employees 1 month after the commencement of operations, all of them nationals. A further requirement, amongst others, is that the business has a turnover of at least 100 times income per capita in that country and has start-up capital of 10 times income per capita at the end of 2009, paid in cash.

3. As we shall see shortly, although Egypt performs well on this measure, it performs much less well on others – thus explaining its overall low rank position.

4. Greene and Storey (2008) point to UK government estimates that policy costs are approximately GBP 8 billion, which is approximately the same public expenditure as devoted to the Police and rather more than is spent on Universities. Estimates of costs using a similar methodology were being undertaken in Sweden by IPREG in 2012 and the early indications are that expenditure per capita in Sweden is broadly similar to that in the United Kingdom.

5. The OECD SME Working Party identified seven headings under which policies can be assessed. These are: Rationale, Additionality, Appropriateness, Superiority, Systemic Efficiency, Own Efficiency and Adaptive Efficiency [OECD, 2000].

Bibliography

Ahmad, N. and A. Hoffmann (2008), "A Framework for Addressing and Measuring Entrepreneurship", *Statistics Working Paper*, OECD, Paris.

Baumol, W.J. (1990), "Entrepreneurship: Productive, Unproductive and Destructive", *Journal of Political Economy*, Vol. 98, No. 5, pp. 893-921.

Dennis, W. (2004), *Creating and sustaining a viable small business sector*, Paper presented at the School of Continuing Education, University of Oklahoma, 27 October.

Gentry, W.M. and R.G. Hubbard (2000), "Tax Policy and Entrepreneurial Entry", *American Economic Review*, 90 (2), pp. 283-287.

INSEAD (2011), *Global Innovation Index Rankings*, INSEAD, Paris.

Greene, F.J., K.M. Mole and D.J. Storey (2008), *Three decades of enterprise culture: Entrepreneurship, economic regeneration and public policy*, Palgrave, New York.

Hoffman, A., D. Koch and D.J. Storey (2010), *Theory and Practice of entrepreneurship policy: Gazelle-hunting by government*, University of Sussex, Brighton.

International Communication Union (2010), *Measuring the Information Society*, ICU.

Geneva, Lundstrom, A., P. Vikstrom, M. Fink, H. Crinjs, P. Glodek, D.J. Storey and A. Kroksgard (2012), "Estimating the cost of Entrepreneurship policy: Cross country approaches in Sweden, Poland, Austria, UK and the Flanders region of Belgium", *IPREG Working Paper*, IPREG, Stockholm.

McCormick, B. and J. Wahba (2001), "Overseas Work Experience, Savings and Entrepreneurship Amongst Return Migrants to LDCs", *Scottish Journal of Political Economy*, 48(2), pp. 164-178.

OECD (2011), *Stratégie de développement du climat des affaires : Maroc 2010*, OECD, Paris.

OECD (2010), *Business Climate Development Review: Egypt 2010*, OECD, Paris.

OECD (2007), *OECD Framework for the Evaluation of SME and Entrepreneurship Policies and Programmes*, OECD, Paris.

Oldsman, E. and K. Hallberg (2002), "Framework for Evaluating the Impact of Small Enterprise Initiatives", in Robinson, K.L., R.D. Christy and N. Baharani (eds.), *Rural Community Economic Development*, pp. 137-168.

Rocha, R., S. Farazi, R. Khouri, and D. Pearce (2011), "The Status of Bank Lending to SMEs in the Middle East and North Africa Region", *World Bank Policy research Working Paper*, No. 5607.

Saxenian, A.L. (2000), "Silicon Valley's New Immigrant Entrepreneurs", *Working Paper* 15, The Center for Comparative Immigration Studies, University of California, Santa Cruz.

Stevenson L (2010), *Private Sector and Enterprise Development: Fostering Growth in the Middle East and North Africa*, Edward Elgar and International Development Research Centre, London and Ottawa.

World Bank (2012), *Ease Of Doing Business Survey*, The World Bank, Washington, DC.

Chapter 5

Rationale and policies to promote high growth enterprises

This chapter summarises the main findings and recommendations of the report. It draws on the conclusions of the previous chapters and puts forth two main sets of policy priorities: measures to improve the overall business environment and targeted measures to support high growth enterprises. Specific policies relate in particular to access to finance, skills development, fostering the participation of women in the economy, improving infrastructure and public services and notably removing obstacles to enterprise creation and competition.

Why focus on young and high impact enterprises in MENA?

Recent applied work on enterprise demography conducted by the OECD and by independent researchers shows that a very small proportion of firms are directly responsible for a high proportion of job creation over time. These enterprises may be "high growth", "high impact", "high performance", "high potential" or, more simply, "gazelles". As well as their direct employment contribution, such enterprises also exercise competitive pressure on the other enterprises operating in the same markets, forcing them to review the way they conduct their activities, and providing additional impact on the productivity and performance of the economy. For all these reasons such enterprises are of great interest to public policy-makers concerned with economic and social issues.

Almost all of the research conducted on enterprise demography has, so far, been undertaken in OECD countries, reflecting the availability of comprehensive time-series micro-data, but there are indications that similar enterprise dynamic patterns are present in countries with very different levels of economic development. High growth or high-performance enterprises appear to be present in nearly all economies, but their share of the entire population of enterprises, their absolute performance and their impact on the economy as a whole varies considerably between countries.

The MENA economies share two features:

● a severe shortage of jobs for a fast-growing population; and

● an associated need to modernise their economies.

Young high-impact enterprises have the potential to influence both of these. The central theme of this report is the role of public policy in promoting and supporting young high potential enterprises.

Other factors also have an impact on enterprise growth, such as macro-economic stability, the level of aggregate demand, the quality of the broad legal and regulatory framework, the extent of contract enforcement and the balance between transparency and corruption. The central theme of this report is the role of all these elements of public policy in promoting and supporting young high potential enterprises.

The analysis in this study is based on the Global Entrepreneurship Monitor (GEM) database and in-depth interviews with the owners and founders of 20 individuals owning young enterprises that could be classified as high-potential or high growth in five MENA countries (Egypt, Jordan, Morocco, Tunisia and the UAE).

The GEM provides a wealth of information about enterprises and their owners and managers for 72 countries, including ten from MENA. The data is used to compare young enterprises in MENA with other economic regions and within the three MENA sub-regions: North West Africa, Middle East and the Gulf. The GEM survey data provides comparable data on enterprises at different stages of the firm life course for a number of countries, including a majority of those in the MENA region, thus addressing the problem of a lack of harmonised enterprise demographic data from official sources for the region.

The interviews with the 20 MENA entrepreneurs add a vital qualitative dimension to the analysis. They constitute a virtual focus group, providing a nuanced understanding of the motivations, aspirations, opportunities and obstacles faced by such entrepreneurs.

This evidence from both sources contributes to a review of public policy in MENA countries wanting to increase the economic and social contribution of young enterprises. There is a distinction between young enterprises and young entrepreneurs. The GEM data confirms that a very large proportion of young enterprises are owned by young entrepreneurs but not exclusively so in the MENA region. Indeed, the interviews reveal that experience, knowledge of market opportunities, contacts and financial resources in the start-up phase are critical factors behind the success of high growth enterprises; these skills and qualities can only be acquired over time.

What we know about young and high impact enterprises in MENA

The MENA region has a lower enterprise prevalence rate than other emerging economic areas, including Latin America and low/medium income Asia. This means that the region has a smaller stock of entrepreneurial activity compared with other dynamic emerging economies.

Fewer enterprises appear to reach the mature stage than in other regions. One possible explanation for this is that the business and regulatory environment prevalent in the MENA region, may favour incumbents over new entrants, particularly in the Gulf and in the Middle East sub-regions.

The new enterprise prevalence rate in the MENA region is about one standard deviation below the global average. Two factors appear to be associated with this relative shortfall.

Most important is the low rate of female participation in the labour force. Of those that do, a large proportion of females work in the public sector. Compared with women elsewhere, and particularly in the developing countries, women in the MENA region have less opportunity to acquire business experience, develop commercial and financial contacts, and are poorly situated to identify promising business opportunities. As MENA women are less involved in the nascent phase of the firm life course, they are also less involved in the stages that follow; infant, young, and mature firms. There is, however, considerable variation in the participation rates by women across the three MENA sub-regions. Their participation as nascent entrepreneurs is highest in the North West African region, where it approaches 50%. It is much lower in the Middle East and Gulf regions, particularly at the latter stages of the firm life course; women comprise only 10% of the owners of mature firms in the Middle East and Gulf regions compared with 30% in North West Africa.

The second major factor associated with lower firm creation is a high rate of population growth reflecting high internal birth rates associated with lower participation of women in the labour force.

An emphasis on traditional values is associated with more firm creation. The MENA region has a very strong emphasis (one and a half standard deviations above the world average) on traditional values. Such an emphasis may be associated with participation in interdependent family, community, or tribal groups that compensate for a reduced government presence. The importance of these factors is confirmed by the interviews with the 20 entrepreneurs. Family members are the second most frequent providers of seed financing, after personal savings, with close personal contacts and community attitudes being generally supportive of entrepreneurship activity.

Nevertheless even this relatively reduced pool generates high potential-enterprises, at a rate that is above that of other emerging economies. The share of high-potential firms in the total enterprise population is also in line with that of other economic groupings. High-potential enterprises comprise between 10 and 20 per cent of all active businesses, depending on the chosen indicator. However this proportion falls markedly once actual employment growth rates are used.

This is because most enterprises in the MENA region are in traditionally low-growth sectors, notably the consumer-oriented services sectors such as retailing, catering, repairing, shops. The potentially more dynamic business service sector is significantly under-represented in the MENA region.

Nevertheless the GEM data and the in-depth interviews show that the pattern of entrepreneurial activity in the MENA region is changing. There are indications that a new generation of young enterprises is emerging that are qualitatively and quantitatively different from the previous generation.

The GEM data indicates these new entrepreneurs are more educated than those managing and owning more established businesses. The share of entrepreneurs with graduate experience leading nascent and infant enterprises is particularly high when compared with other emerging economies and is comparable to high-income countries. They are also much more driven by opportunity than by necessity. Women comprise a larger proportion of nascent entrepreneurs, particularly in the North West African region, compared with established firm owners, suggesting that women are now more involved than in previous years. The GEM data also shows that young enterprises have a higher job-generation potential in MENA than more established enterprises and therefore may play a more prominent role in job creation.

A generational change may, thus, be under way. However progress is slow and it will be some time before there are major changes to the profile of the typical young enterprise in MENA countries.

For instance, in the North West African sub-region, the profile of the average young enterprise continues to be that of a micro-enterprise established by a youthful poorly educated individual, driven more by necessity than opportunity and operating in the traditional sectors. High-potential enterprises are real outliers, in the sub-region, but the enterprise creation rate is healthy and a new generation of women entrepreneurs is emerging.

This pattern is repeated in the Middle East sub-region. Where it differs is that the share of women entrepreneurs is lower, but new entrepreneurs are on average more educated than in North West Africa. Nascent enterprises seem to face higher entry barriers and the actual rate of business creation is comparatively low. However the market impact of high-potential enterprises is higher and the number of enterprises active in sectors with a higher technological profile is proportionally larger than in North West Africa.

The profile of the typical enterprise in the Gulf countries is very different. It is a well-established business, run by an older male who is well connected and relatively well-educated and is focussed on business opportunities. Its position is hardly challenged by new entrants. Well-established enterprises seem in the best position to take advantage of new business opportunities and show the highest growth potential and have greater market impact than new entrants.

Despite the superficial stability in these patterns there are also important changes taking place. This is because there are more young people benefitting from higher education and from the modernisation of the MENA economies. This creates the opportunity to exploit the emergence of a higher value business services sector and the growing number of quality-conscious consumers. The interviews used in the study emphasise that many of the respondents have made the transition from a high-potential to a high growth enterprise. The rewards they have reaped, both in terms of personal satisfaction and financial returns are significant, although the obstacles they had to surmount were considerable and the risks they took were high.

What can public policy do to promote and foster high growth enterprises?

If young, high growth enterprises are so important for achieving growth and generating additional and higher quality jobs, what can government do to promote their creation, increase their number and foster their development?

Chapter 4 notes the experience of OECD countries where SME development policies have been in place, in some cases, for decades.

The first lesson that emerges is that there is no "one size fits all" approach, and countries have a series of policy choices open to them. However, experience shows that effective policies are Coherent, have Objectives, Targets and place considerable weight upon Evaluation. In other words, they satisfy the requirements of the COTE Framework.

There are two sets of policy priorities. The first are improvements to the business environment; the second are policies specifically targeted at high impact enterprises.

All private, profit-driven, but not rent-seeking, enterprises will benefit from an improvement in the business environment. However, it is high impact enterprises that are likely to benefit disproportionately from the removal of obstacles to growth and competition, since it is these obstacles that currently impair their development.

High growth enterprises are likely to benefit most from the removal of obstacles to growth and competition.

Five improvements to the businesses environment are needed:

- Regulatory policy and regulatory simplification to establish a transparent regulatory framework, in order to increase competition in the business sector.
- Increase competition and diversification in the banking and financial sectors.
- Policies to increase women's participation in the labour market and in enterprise creation.
- Legal and judiciary reform to improve contract enforcement.
- Human capital development policies to improve skills and promote an entrepreneurial culture.

Attention to these issues would signal to existing and potential entrepreneurs that the governments of MENA countries are serious about including the private sector in realising their economic growth potential, hence raising the interest of potential entrepreneurs with relevant knowledge and experience to engage in entrepreneurial activities. Governments that act on these five issues would be placing the quality of the business environment at the heart of SME and entrepreneurship policy.

The second set of policy recommendations is less straightforward and calls for selective government interventions to promote and support high-impact enterprises. In addition, they are more problematic because of the difficulties in accurately identifying the target group: the high-impact or high-potential enterprise. Nonetheless, it is vital to ensure that MENA countries provide an economic environment in which high impact-enterprises can thrive.

Targeted support for high-impact enterprises can also be distilled into five priority areas.

The inability to **access finance** can be a major constraint upon enterprise growth. The most notable examples are those in the high-tech sectors, where "front-end" research and development is required some time before there are sales and profits.

External equity financing, either provided by business angels, seed funds, venture capital or equity funds, found in many OECD countries is, with the partial exception of UAE, scarce in the region. To address this shortcoming, governments in the MENA region can draw on the experience of several OECD governments and the European Union, where programmes such as the European Seed Capital Fund or the US Small Business Investment Company (SBIC) encourage the private sector to supply equity. Once such funding becomes established it then appears to stimulate an entire supporting eco-system comprising auditors, specialised lawyers, investment advisors, fund managers, investment funds and stock markets for low capitalised companies.

In practice, however even in developed countries, external equity is not the main source of funding even for fast-growth firms. Instead, the key is access to bank credit on appropriate terms and conditions. The case-study interviews reveal that such access is difficult in MENA countries. High growth firms in OECD countries use a diversity of funding sources, including asset-based finance, term loans, overdrafts, overnight funding, leasing, factoring, hire-purchase and even personal credit cards. The task of governments is to ensure that these sources are provided by financial institutions in marketplaces that are competitive. In addition, publicly-funded credit agencies, present in most of the MENA countries, should introduce special schemes tailored to the needs of high potential/high growth enterprises, in line with the recommendations made by the OECD. As an example, Kafalat, the Lebanese credit guarantee agency has already introduced a facility for high growth and high-tech enterprises.

A second important area for targeted policies is **skills development**. The case studies highlight how high growth enterprises in MENA countries find it difficult to attract skilled employees. At the same time, entrepreneurs often complain that existing, publicly funded training schemes, even when available, are often too generic and not tailored to their specific needs. Governments therefore should consider developing instruments to respond to the often highly specific requirements of high growth or high-potential enterprises. Examples of such custom-fit programmes could include: voucher schemes that would allow specific types of enterprises to select the trainers or advisors and at the same time to have part to the cost covered by public funds; the joint development of internship programmes with universities and vocational institutes; and the establishment of hiring programmes for new graduates, supported by tax credits or temporary government grants. Central to any programme of skills development are the universities and, given that all of our case-study firms have graduate owners, these links need to be more strongly developed. This may be in the form of the development of science parks, but more widely governments should encourage the engagement of students working for periods of time in small and micro-enterprises. Such programmes can benefit both the student and the enterprise.

In the OECD countries, many high growth enterprises are operating in the advanced business services sector (ITC, consultancy and accounting services, logistic, finance, human resources, etc.). This sector is relatively under-developed in the MENA region. The demand for advanced business services often originates from Multi-National Enterprises (MNEs), which indicates that there should be a focus on strengthening links between local high-potential service enterprises and MNEs.

In addition to the above two areas of intervention, there are three others, more horizontal in nature, that will enhance the development of high growth and high-potential enterprises. The **low participation of women** in the labour force, as a whole, is a major determinant of the entrepreneurial gender gap. Although an increasing number of women in MENA countries are now able to access higher education, they remain largely marginalised in the labour market and confined to traditional business sectors or to public administration. In designing training and internship programmes, governments should pursue an active gender policy. This might include subsidising enterprises hiring a qualified female intern/employee. In this way, women will be able to obtain the relevant business training and experience outside the traditional sectors, opening up opportunities to develop a professional career and perhaps to start their own business venture.

A second priority horizontal policy area for government is the provision of **reliable and low cost public services**. High-potential firms are strongly disadvantaged by poor public services such as ITC, transport infrastructure, electricity and water supply, since they are heavy users of these services.

Finally, governments need to pursue an active policy to **remove obstacles to business entry**, by creating a level playing field and fostering competition, particularly in sectors that present opportunities for growth. This requires systematic action, reviewing the sector regulatory framework at national and local levels, current competition and business practices, public procurement practices, rules and regulations governing professional bodies, and how these rules are enforced. Unfair competition, either from the informal sector or from the abuse of dominant market positions, has to be eradicated and replaced by fair competition. This alone will do most to transform marketplaces by creating conditions favourable for high growth and high-potential enterprises, thus lifting the performance of the MENA economies.

Although the case for supporting high growth and high-potential enterprises is compelling there are no guarantees that all elements of this policy will see immediate returns. Indeed, it is likely that some will be more successful than others. Governments may also be criticised for allocating resources to support only a small section of the SME population.

Closely monitored pilot projects with clearly defined targets and objectives, can help to address this problem. The policy impact of such projects must be assessedby taking into account the opinions of all involved parties and by methodical evaluation. Governments should then be ready to make consequent policy adjustments.

The MENA region at the end of the first decade of the new millennium is undergoing significant political and institutional change. There is no way of knowing where this change will take the region, but what is clear is that it creates an opportunity to re-think the design and implementation of entrepreneurship and SME policies. The changes underway may lead to a more open dialogue between the government and the business community that would permit wider policy experimentation through a more pragmatic and evidence-based approach. It is an historical opportunity not to be missed.

ORGANISATION FOR ECONOMIC CO-OPERATION AND DEVELOPMENT

The OECD is a unique forum where governments work together to address the economic, social and environmental challenges of globalisation. The OECD is also at the forefront of efforts to understand and to help governments respond to new developments and concerns, such as corporate governance, the information economy and the challenges of an ageing population. The Organisation provides a setting where governments can compare policy experiences, seek answers to common problems, identify good practice and work to co-ordinate domestic and international policies.

The OECD member countries are: Australia, Austria, Belgium, Canada, Chile, the Czech Republic, Denmark, Estonia, Finland, France, Germany, Greece, Hungary, Iceland, Ireland, Israel, Italy, Japan, Korea, Luxembourg, Mexico, the Netherlands, New Zealand, Norway, Poland, Portugal, the Slovak Republic, Slovenia, Spain, Sweden, Switzerland, Turkey, the United Kingdom and the United States. The European Commission takes part in the work of the OECD.

OECD Publishing disseminates widely the results of the Organisation's statistics gathering and research on economic, social and environmental issues, as well as the conventions, guidelines and standards agreed by its members.

CANADA'S INTERNATIONAL DEVELOPMENT RESEARCH CENTRE

A key part of Canada's aid program, IDRC supports research in developing countries to promote growth and development. IDRC also encourages sharing this knowledge with policymakers, other researchers, and communities around the world. The result is innovative, lasting local solutions that aim to bring change to those who need it most.

OECD PUBLISHING, 2, rue André-Pascal, 75775 PARIS CEDEX 16
(25 2013 04 1 P) ISBN 978-92-64-10025-1 – No. 60293 2013-02

THE MOUNTAINS OF SN

THE LANDSCAPE PHOTOGRAPHY OF

JOHN CLOW

CREATIVE MONOCHROME
CONTEMPORARY PORTFOLIO SERIES

JOHN CLOW is a native of Rothwell in North-amptonshire, where he has lived all his life, except for seven years when serving in the Royal Navy. His passion for walking and climbing in Snowdonia extends over 30 years, during which time he has used his technical expertise and enthusiasm for monochrome photography and painting to record and interpret the ever changing beauty of the wild cwms (valleys).

A Fellow of the Royal Photographic Society and a member of the Rushden and District Photographic Society, John is a well known lecturer in camera clubs throughout the country, travelling selflessly to show his work and share his enthusiasm.

He has held five one-man exhibitions in the UK and was invited in 1989 to exhibit his work in Russia. His work has also been seen in many national and international salons and has received numerous awards, including a Gold Medal in the Barcelona Salon during the Olympic Games for a panel of mountain scenes taken, of course, in Snowdonia.

THE MOUNTAINS OF SNOWDONIA
The landscape photography of
JOHN CLOW

Published in the UK by Creative Monochrome
20 St Peters Road, Croydon, Surrey, CR0 1HD.
© Creative Monochrome, 1993.

British Library Cataloguing-in-Publication Data:
A catalogue record for this book is available from
the British Library

ISBN 1 873319 08 8
First edition, 1993

Printed in England by The Bath Press,
Lower Bristol Road, Bath.

FOREWORD

JENIFER ROBERTS

The mountains of Snowdonia, known in Welsh as *Eryri* ('the place of eagles'), have inspired this atmospheric collection of photographs by John Clow. John is in love with these mountains. He has climbed them and walked amongst them for over 30 years.

His pictures depict the beauty and the bleakness. the wind and the cold. He is an artist responding to the mountains, to the quality of light and weather upon the land and, perhaps most of all, to the wind. It is the wind that creates many of John's images as the clouds move across the sky during long time exposures (courtesy of a powerful neutral density filter).

In the BBC radio programme, *The Tingle Factor,* people talk about the pieces of music that, for them, produce the elusive tingle that shows that something in the music has bypassed their conscious mind and is affecting their sub-conscious, their emotions, directly. The tingle factor can apply to any creative medium, but it cannot be forced. It comes unexpectedly, when visiting art galleries, reading poetry, listening to music.

I have seen individual photographs by John Clow over the years but, until asked to write this foreword, I had not seen his Snowdonia series in its entirety. Leafing through the prints, I became aware that they rate highly on my own tingle factor. I felt as if I was standing on the same mountainside, as if I too was leaning into the wind, watching the clouds move across the sky. It is John's spirit, the part of him that also paints and writes poetry, that is moved by the elements, by the combination of landscape and weather that inspires him to take these photographs.

It is the same part of him that, in the darkroom, creates prints that reveal this personal response to the viewer. This is the true art of photography. A straight print of any of these photographs would not express the deep emotion that John feels about his subject. Prints can only reveal the spirit of the photographer if they are made with great care and subtlety, with feeling and with passion. And, of course, if they are printed by the photographer himself.

Ansel Adams, the photographer that John Clow admires above all others, made the well-known musical analogy: that the negative is the score and the print the performance. As in music, the interpretation of the negative depends on the personality of the printer. It follows that, if photographers are to make a truly personal statement, they must do their own printing. If the prints are made by someone else, then the photographer's unique vision is diluted by the influence of another personality, however skilled the second person may be as a printer.

Why are so few people aware of this craft, the skill and techniques required to make a fine photographic print? Most non-photographers, even those who are highly visually aware, have no idea how a fine print is made. I know too many people who love paintings, music and poetry but who would never dream of going to see a photographic exhibition, let alone buy a photographic print. A variety of different techniques are used to create other types of original print, such as lithographs, screenprints and woodcuts, and I see no reason why the methods used to produce photographic prints should be considered of lesser value. Photography is just another form of creativity and creating a fine photographic print in the darkroom is just another method of printmaking.

In any field of artistic endeavour, the message is more important than the medium. John Clow uses photography as his medium but his message in these photographs, his deeply felt response to the mountains of Snowdonia, could equally well be made in other media. Yet the expression of the artist's spirit, his response to the elements that inspire him, can only be communicated to others if he has honed his skills in his chosen medium to a high level of craftsmanship. John has been taking photographs of Snowdonia for many years and has spent countless days in the darkroom, teasing out the best from his negatives. His skills behind the camera and as a printer allow us to share some of the excitement and sense of wonder that these mountains arouse in him.

In critical circles today, a photographer's intellect is valued more highly than his spirit. While the best work can affect both the heart and the mind, I feel strongly that the purpose of art is to affect the emotions first. The intellect can be stimulated by so many other things in our modern world. Reading a book by an art historian recently, I came across the words "what was the artist thinking when he created this work?". But the artist was almost certainly not thinking, he was feeling, and if people do not understand that,

then they fail to understand the true nature of the creative process. So much of creativity is spiritual and viewers who approach work only from an intellectual viewpoint will miss a great deal.

This collection of photographs is an evocation of the many moods of Snowdonia, filtered through the personality of John Clow. Those who look for intellectual content in photography will be disappointed in this book, but those who respond to the poetic in nature will be enriched. These photographs not only capture the spirit of Snowdonia but, more importantly, they also capture the spirit of John Clow as he walks in the mountains that he has loved for so long.

JENIFER ROBERTS *is an acclaimed professional landscape photographer and the author of* Spirit of the Place*, published in 1992 by Creative Monochrome.*

TO SNOWDONIA

*When I have gone the song will remain,
the wind and the rain, the mists.
The poetry of time endless
unyielding.*

John Clow

"I didn't see you on the bus." I looked round in surprise to see a perfect stranger. "I haven't been on a bus," I replied. I discovered that the confusion arose from the blue No. 8 shirt I was wearing, which I had retained when demobbed from the Navy a few months earlier. My new companion was one of a team of Royal Navy climbers staying in the Ogwen Valley, and naturally assumed that I belonged to that party.

We were seated on the summit of Tryfan on a glorious Sunday morning in April; the sky was blue and the air was fresh. I enquired of his friends and was told that they were climbing the mountain by the 'Grooved Arete', 'Pinnacle Ribs' and 'Gashed Crag' and so forth. He had walked up the easy way because he had sprained his wrist the previous day. We chatted for some time before he departed, leaving me intrigued by a world of grooved aretes and gashed crags and with a determination to seek out this world of mysterious highways among the mountains.

The year was 1958 and I had driven to Snowdonia on an old two-stroke twin which tended to seize up when the speedo' indicated 60 mph. I found accommodation on the Friday evening at a guest house in Capel Curig. I woke on the Saturday to find low clouds obscuring the hills. Being a perfect stranger to the area, I enquired at breakfast where a novice might go in safety in the hills on such a day. I was introduced to the landlord, who luckily was a local guide, and was advised that I might enjoy such a day in Cwm Idwal and probably walk up to the Devil's Kitchen if the clouds were not too low. His instructions were precise and offered generously, adding that if the weather worsened I should beat a hasty retreat and, in any case, be back for dinner at seven sharp.

I found my way up to the Devil's Kitchen and sat at its base for some time, gazing in awe at the gaping chasm which disappeared up into the clouds. It was three in the afternoon: kick-off time at the local football match back home, where I usually spent my Saturday afternoons. I cast such mundane thoughts aside, reflecting that I had discovered a far better world of silence and of the mystery of what hid above the curtain of cloud a few feet above my head. I sat there for quite a long time enjoying this new experience until a little voice reminded me of my recall for dinner at seven sharp.

Dinner was not quite what I had expected: it was a huge feast of home cooking – they had obviously catered for mountainous appetites before. Dinner over, I sought out the landlord for advice for the morrow. He advised me that the weather was improving and, should the clouds clear, I could attempt the ascent of Tryfan, but only by the easiest route from Ogwen Cottage.

Magic. Sunday dawned clear and fine. After breakfast I travelled along the A5 road and parked my motorcycle at Ogwen and made my way to the rocky summit of Tryfan, carefully following my prescribed route via Llyn Bochlwyd. Seated on the sun-warmed rocks which lay around in profusion at the feet of Adam and Eve, those two rock obelisks which cap the summit and are so clearly seen on a fine day from the A5 road, I made my chance acquaintance with this stranger from the Royal Navy whose remarks were to lead me on a quest to seek out these wild places. A new world of adventure and beauty, previously unbeknown and undreamt of, was to unroll before my eyes in the coming years.

On returning home, my mind was made up. The habits of a short lifetime were about to experience an abrupt change. It was love at first sight and the mountains had won. The next decade found my life engrossed in rock climbing, impatiently awaiting the next vertical problem. The passing years and ageing limbs eventually demanded more rest; the pace slackened and more time was spent admiring the ever-changing beauty of the wild cwms. I had started to carry a camera and attempted to record the inexhaustible beauty that surrounded me.

My photographic technique has evolved over the years to enable me to capture not only what I see, but what I feel: my emotion at the time of releasing the shutter.

My negatives record the information that appears in the viewfinder. Within limits, by using filters, I can exercise a little control over the values of tonal areas. Adjustment of aperture is usually to influence depth of field, with the shutter speed being varied where I need to give the impression of movement. There is no such thing as the perfect exposure: it is almost aways a compromise. I always use a tripod, but very rarely focus a landscape, relying instead on the hyperfocal characteristics of the lens in use.

In the darkroom, tonal areas of the print are fine-tuned to produce the emphasis which will determine the quality of the final statement. This is achieved by the age old method of burning-in and holding back. Modern variable contrast printing papers have added another dimension to the possibilities of contrast control on one sheet of paper.

The path from first visualising the image to the final print is often complex, but always fascinating and exciting; when Ansel Adams was once asked if he had taken the perfect picture, he answered that it was like prosperity – just round the corner.

My camera has been the catalyst between myself and my chosen subject; the images before you in this portfolio are the vehicles of communication with yourselves.

The mountains of Snowdonia have been my chosen inspiration, not because I consider them more photogenic than any other place, but, among other reasons, because I was fortunate in finding a home-from-home in the Llanberis Pass above the lovely village of Nant Peris. The ever-open door, roaring fire and ready welcome were not to be ignored. The mountains rise steeply from the doorway and are prey to the south-westerly gales that batter their ramparts incessantly. But it is the ephemeral quality of light, the transparent mist and impenetrable rain that has held me spellbound longer than I care to remember. In the quiet moments, the mountains speak of the timeless restlessness of nature, but only in a whisper – words carried on the wild winds of eternity.

DEDICATION

This portfolio is dedicated
to the memory of Mrs Smith who shared her home,
Coed Gwydr above Nant Peris, and her love
of the mountains so generously
for so many years.

TO CWM IDWAL

Silent hollow, dark foreboding,
a whisper stirs the silence,
sunlight drifts across the water sparkling
and ascends the cold, grey rocks, 'tis gone.
The mist creeps down embracing,
the spirit rests,
eternity is there to touch.

1.
Distant Idwal
Cwm Idwal

2.
Hill and mist
Glyder Fawr and Llyn Idwal

3.
Fleeting sunlight
Llyn Idwal

4.
Where no birds fly
Llyn Idwal

TO SILENCE

To feel the silence, is to meet a friend
by placid waters that reflect the soul
and thoughts of days departed long ago.

5.
Space and time
Llyn Caseg-fraith

6.
Dawn reflections
Llyn Gwynant and Yr Aran

7.
Winter dawn
Llynau Mymbyr and Snowdon

8.
Reflections
Llyn Bochlwyd

To The Waters

Clear waters gliding, foaming
to the seas from whence they came.
Through rock and heather, over steepening falls
to join the silver flood of destiny.

9.
The shallows
Afon Glaslyn

10. (top)
Cascade
Afon Las, Llanberis Pass

11. (below)
In spate
Afon Ogwen

12. (top)
Waterworn
Aber falls

13. (below)
Time flow
Afon Cwmllan

14.
In flood
Afon Llugwy

To The Clouds

They drift across the waiting mountain tops,
an everchanging tapestry of form
so full of beauty.
In their dark caverns carry snow and rain
to give us life, their life so short.

15.
Menace
Cwm Clogwyn Du'r Arddu

16. (top)
To windward
Yr Wyddfa, south ridge

17. (below)
The Cauldron
Above Cwm Dyli

18. (top)
Stormclouds
Towards Tryfan and The Glyders

19. (below)
Spring shower
Llyn Idwal and the Ogwen Valley

21

20. *(top)*
Cloudscape
Above the Ogwen Valley

21. *(below)*
To the north
Towards Tryfan and The Carneddau

TO THE WIND

The restless winds carry the mists
of time over high ridges
and into silent cwms.
They murmur of the unknown
in their passage across the landscape,
the endless transience of infinity.

22.
Sou' westerly
Llynau Mymbyr and Snowdon

23. (top)
Wind and ridge
The pinnacles of Crib Goch

24. (below)
Traeth mists
Towards Snowdon from Dyffryn

24

25. (top)
Passage of silence
Above Gallt yr Ogof

26. (below)
Above the pass
Llanberis Pass

27. (top)
Woodland and wind
Near Llyn Dinas

28. (below)
The clamour of Spring
Towards Craig yr Ysfa

TO WINTER

Cold fingers hold the landscape
in a vice like grip, the streams are stilled
and on the hillside nothing moves.
A land of quiet white and greys,
so cold and so immediate
that even time stands still.

29.
The ice garden
Llyn Gwynant and Yr Aran

30.
Stilled waters
Afon Peris above Nant Peris

31.
Frozen landscape
Llyn Du'r Arddu

32.
Snowclouds and sunlight
Llyn Gwynant and Yr Aran

33.
Sculptured by the wind
Moel Siabod

34.
The hard life
Below Braich Llwyd

TO LIGHT

A moment passes whilst nature changes
the mundane to the ethereal.
That fleeting touch
the benediction of light.

35.
After the rain
Yr Elen and The Carneddau

36.
Hillside pasture
Cwm Patrig, Llanberis Pass

37.
Rock and sheep
Cwm Patrig, Llanberis Pass

38.
Afterglow
Snowdon and Llynau Mymbyr

39.
Curtain call
Lliwedd from Dyffryn

40.
Evening sunlight
Yr Elen and The Carneddau

TO SNOWDONIA

When I have gone the song will remain,
the wind and the rain, the mists.
The poetry of time endless
unyielding.

41.
The unequal struggle
Tal-y-braich-Uchaf, Ogwen Valley

42. (top)
Sea of mist
Above the Nant Francon Pass

43. (below)
The castle of the winds
Castell y Gwynt

44. *(top)*
Mist and rain
Crib Goch

45. *(below)*
Storm clouds
Tryfan, Ogwen Valley

46. *(top)*
Quiet landscape
Llyn Ffynnon Lloer

47. *(below)*
Wild Wales
Above Tal-y-Llyn-Ogwen

48. (top)
The Devil's Kitchen
Twll Du, Cwm Idwal

49. (below)
Hill and cloud
Above Y Gribin, Ogwen Valley

50.
Sunlight and rock
Cwm Idwal and Pen Yr Olewen

51.
Distant peak
Pen Llithrig-y-Wrach

52.
Passing storm
Above Nanmor

46

53.
There's a long, long road
Snowdon from Dyffryn

PHOTOGRAPHIC DATA

Ref	Month	Lens (mm)	Filter*	Aperture	Shutter speed	Paper grade	Ref	Month	Lens (mm)	Filter*	Aperture	Shutter speed	Paper grade
1	Oct	80	O	f/16	1/15	3	27	Oct	80	O, ND	f/22	2 min	3.5
2	Oct	80	O, ND	f/22	2 min	4.5	28	May	80	R, ND	f/22	4 min	3, 4.5
3	Oct	80	O	f/22	1/15	3.5	29	Jan	80	–	f/22	1/15	1.5, 3.5
4	Oct	50	ND	f/22	8 sec	4	30	Feb	80	–	f/11	1/125	1.5
5	Sep	80	–	f/8	1/125	3	31	Mar	80	–	f/5.6	1/125	3.5
6	Oct	80	O	f/22	1/15	2, 4.5	32	Jan	50	–	f/16	1/30	3, 4.5
7	Feb	80	O	f/22	1/8	2, 5	33	Feb	50	–	f/16	1/125	4.5
8	Sep	80	R	f/22	1/2	4	34	Feb	80	–	f/11	1/30	3
9	Oct	80	O, ND	f/22	10 min	4	35	May	80	R	f/8	1/30	4
10	Mar	80	R, P	f/22	1/2	3.5	36	Nov	150	–	f/16	1/30	3
11	May	50	–	f/5.6	1/30	3.5	37	Nov	150	–	f/16	1/15	4
12	Nov	80	–	f/11	1 sec	3.5	38	Feb	80	–	f/22	1/15	5
13	Sep	150	–	f/22	1/2	4	39	Oct	150	R	f/8	1/30	5
14	Nov	80	–	f/16	30 sec	4	40	Dec	150	R	f/8	1/60	5
15	Mar	80	R	f/5.6	1/30	3	41	Sep	150	R	f/11	1/8	2, 4.5
16	Sep	80	O	f/8	1/60	3, 5	42	Sep	80	R	f/11	1/30	4.5
17	Oct	80	O	f/16	1/15	3.5, 5	43	Nov	150	O	f/11	1/60	2, 4.5
18	Jan	80	R	f/4	1/250	3.5, 5	44	Jun	38	–	f/5.6	1/125	4.5
19	May	38	R	f/11	1/30	3.5, 5	45	Mar	80	–	f/8	1/125	4
20	Jun	80	R	f/8	1/60	3.5	46	Aug	150	–	f/11	1/60	2.5, 5
21	Jun	50	R	f/11	1/30	3	47	Sep	80	–	f/22	1/8	3
22	Jan	38	–	f/22	1/4	2.5, 5	48	Jun	80	–	f/22	1/15	2.5, 5
23	Jun	150	R, ND	f/8	3 min	5	49	May	80	R	f/11	1/30	3.5, 5
24	Oct	80	R, ND	f/8	5 min	5	50	Oct	50	O	f/22	1/8	3.5
25	Sep	80	R, ND	f/22	35 sec	5	51	Oct	50	R	f/22	1/2	4.5
26	Oct	150	R, ND	f/16	2 min	5	52	Dec	80	–	f/11	1/125	3, 4.5
							53	Oct	80	R, ND	f/8	4 min	5

John uses a Hasselblad 500CM camera. All the negatives were made on Ilford FP4 120 roll film and developed in ID11 diluted with an equal part of water. All the prints were made on Ilford Multigrade III RC glossy paper, processed in Ilford Multigrade developer.

*Filters:

R = Red 6x (-2.5 stops)

O = Orange 4x (-2 stops)

ND = Neutral Density 64x (-6 stops)

P = Polarising 2x (-1 stop)

For further details of the Contemporary Portfolio Series and a catalogue of Creative Monochrome publications, please write to Creative Monochrome, 20 St Peters Road, Croydon, Surrey, CR0 1HD

THE DAMS RAID

THROUGH THE LENS

By HELMUTH EULER

Contents

Credits

ISBN: 1 870067 27 4

© Helmuth Euler/*After the Battle*, 2001

Translated by Michael Ockenden

Designed by Winston G. Ramsey, Editor-in-Chief *After the Battle*

PUBLISHERS

Battle of Britain International Limited, Church House, Church Street, London E15 3JA

PRINTERS

Printed in Great Britain by Heronsgate Ltd, Basildon, Essex.

PHOTOGRAPHS

All the photographs are from the author's archive, save for the following:

Australian War Memorial: *Page 224 left.*
Commonwealth War Graves Commission: *Page 92 top left.*
J. A. H van den Driesschen: *Page 216 both.*
Imperial War Museum: *Page 16 right, 17 right, 20 right, 21 left and centre, 23 top left, 24 top right and bottom, 26 left, 27 left, 30 top right, 31, 48 bottom right, 49, 86 right, 97, 111, 158, 159, 160 right, 161 bottom, 162, 163 both, 164 both, 165 both, 166, 167, 168, 208, 209 right, 220.*
Kardar Luftbild: *Page 53.*
University of Keele: *Page 106 left, 108 right.*
Heinz Leiwig: *Page 181 left.*
Lincolnshire Aviation Heritage Centre: *Page 226 bottom.*
Mike McCormac: *Page 51 bottom left and right, 52 top left and right.*
National Physical Laboratory: *Page 19 right.*
Public Record Office: *Page 40, 41.*
Royal Air Force Museum, Hendon: *Page 34 left.*
Royal Air Force, Scampton: *Page 230, 231, 232, 233.*
Winfried von Rüden: *Page 213, 219 left.*
Ruhrverband Essen: *Page 5 right.*
Transport Road Research Laboratory: *Page 10 bottom.*
Ullstein Bilderdienst: *Page 222 top right.*
Wasser und Schiffahrtamt Hannoversch-Münden: *Page 76.*
Werkfoto Preussenelektra: *Page 7 bottom.*

MAPS

Landesvermessungsamt Nordrhein-Westfalen, Bonn.

ENDPAPERS

Front left: The vital Möhne dam, critical for the supply of water and hydro-electric power for the German war machine in the Ruhr, pictured after the attack on the night of May 16/17, 1943. The ruined building in the foreground was the home of Franz Müller which lay some 300 metres from the local inn at Günne run by Adolf Nölle. His story appears on page 120.

Front right: The flooded valley at Guntershausen, some 46 kilometres below the Eder — the second dam attacked that night. Although its importance to German industry was minimal — its main purpose being to regulate water levels — the prestige factor to the Royal Air Force in breaching two of Germany's biggest dams in a single stroke was immeasurable.

Rear left: Although an exact death toll has never been established, around 1,400 people were drowned in the tidal waves which bore down the Möhne and Eder valleys. This is the state funeral for the victims at Neheim (see page 126).

Rear right: Eight of the Lancasters failed to return. RAF casualties were 53 killed in action with three men taken prisoner. These are the graves of the crew of AJ-M in Rheinberg War Cemetery, north of Krefeld (see page 60).

FRONTISPIECE

The Möhne dam before the raid, courtesy of Foto-Dülberg/H. Windgassen, Soest.

REAR COVER

A rare sight — the Möhne dam in full flow with water cascading from the 105 overflow vents. (Photo by the author.)

Introduction

Operation 'Chastise' has become a legend in the annals of military history, possessing as it does the traditional military attributes of originality, surprise and heroism, coupled with a dramatic outcome. In Germany, the victims of the catastrophe have not been forgotten, and following the publication of my book *Als Deutschlands Dämme brachen* in 1975, many German eyewitnesses came forward with additional reports, photographs and film material about the night attacks against the Möhne and Eder dams. Also, with the passage of 50 years, previously-classified records have now been released and other hitherto unknown documents made public which were included in my second book *Wasserkrieg* published in 1992.

During the night of May 16/17, 1943, 19 Lancaster bombers of the RAF's newly-formed No. 617 Squadron launched a low-level attack against four dams in the Ruhr. Within an hour, the special 'bouncing' bombs had smashed two of the main targets, the massive dams in the Möhne and Eder valleys. The Sorpe was damaged but the Ennepe withstood the attack. Eight Lancasters did not return.

Yet though it had been based on a series of experiments whose results had been accurately predicted, the first air raid to have been conceived within the context of engineering technology proved a failure. Its target was the arsenal of the Third Reich but the anticipated strategic advantages for the Allies failed to materialise and production continued unhindered. Even at a time when Britain needed victories in the air — and the operation certainly bolstered British civilian morale — was it worth the cost in time and materials, coupled with the loss of eight bombers and the lives of 53 men?

How did the Royal Air Force manage to breach the Möhne and Eder dams, which together held back 336 million tonnes of water? From an examination of original documents it is clear that the Air Ministry had, in September 1937, already identified German dams and reservoirs as potential targets in any new war, and in October of the same year the Möhne and Sorpe were specifically named. With the outbreak of hostilities in September 1939, RAF Bomber Command concentrated on the notion that if the nerve centre of the German military economy could be paralysed, the war would be shortened considerably.

By the beginning of 1943 many of the RAF's proposals had been put forward, agreed and listed, but with this came the realisation that conventional techniques could not be used to destroy the dams. Tactics such as torpedoes, remote-controlled flying boats filled with explosives, the synchronised detonation of sea mines, or sabotage units dropped by parachute had all been considered for use against the Möhne dam. Initially, Barnes Wallis believed the dams could be brought down with a 10-ton earthquake bomb but in May 1943 such a device was impossible to deliver and drop accurately. Wallis was not the first to recognise the German dams as important targets, but he was the one who came up with the brilliant idea of using a bouncing bomb to unleash the waters pent up behind the Möhne and Eder dams.

Barnes Wallis tinkered with his bomb theories for three years in the face of resistance from aviation experts. When the decision was taken on February 26, 1943 to implement Operation 'Chastise', there were no detailed drawings of the special weapon. No. 617 Squadron, under Wing Commander Guy Gibson, had just seven weeks to practise low-level flying, and the first and only test with a live bomb was successfully carried out only three days before the attack.

The decision to give priority to 'Upkeep' (the dam-busting bomb) over 'Highball' (the anti-surface vessel bomb) was not taken at the Air Ministry in London but in Washington where RAF Chiefs-of-Staff were conferring with their American opposite numbers. The Air Ministry asked for a decision and on May 14 a message from the United States brought the news they had been hoping for — the attack was to go ahead. Two essential factors had to coincide: the required water levels behind the dams and a full moon. The latest possible date when 'Chastise' could successfully be carried out was May 26 for only then would these two criteria exist.

The Dams Raid was undoubtedly Bomber Command's most spectacular operation, of the Second World War, and it has been described by the official British military historian as 'the most precise bombing attack ever delivered and a feat of arms which has never been excelled'.

The scale of the devastation unleashed by a single bomb — in this case 'Upkeep' — was not exceeded until the atomic bomb was dropped on Japan in 1945. During the course of Germany's longest night, over 200 square kilometres of land were flooded and some 1,400 people lost their lives — the highest number to date in an air raid.

This, then, is the story of that attack, graphically told 'through the lenses' of the photographers who recorded the scenes before, during and after the operation.

HELMUTH EULER, 2001

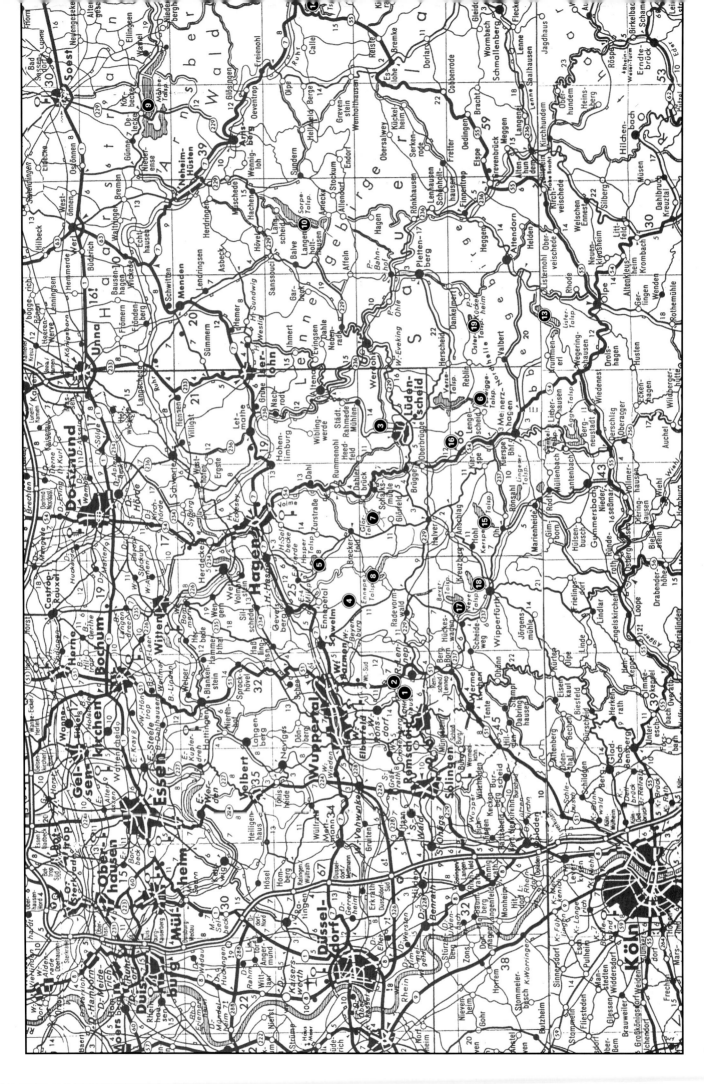

The Möhne, 120 kilometres east of Cologne, was the largest to be completed in the Ruhr.

Dam-building in the Ruhrgebiet

The construction of dams is one of the most important technical achievements of mankind. Engineers have always tried to store water in large quantities, be this to provide drinking water for towns, irrigation for fields during droughts, or the protection of inhabited areas from floods. However, the construction of artificial reservoirs is not an invention of the 19th and 20th centuries and important dams had already been built in ancient times. For thousands of years the building of dams has gone hand in hand with the development of cities, for settlements of any size have always required an adequate supply of water. Contemporary writers tell of 'Lake Moeris' situated in Fayum Oasis, 50 miles south of Cairo where, with the help of dams and canals, a masterpiece of civil engineering stored up the floodwaters of the Nile for use during dry periods; more than 1,800 years BC one of the most fertile provinces of ancient Egypt was created by means of a dam. However, the oldest existing dam is that at Sadd-el-Kafara built 2700-2600 BC in Wadi Garawi 20 miles south of Cairo. Built for protection against flood-water with a 40-foot-high wall, it was destroyed before completion due to an unexpected flood. The remnants can still be seen today.

In Germany, important dam-building works took place in the 16th and 17th centuries in the Harz region where water power was used for smelting and metal processing in the mining industry. Traditional metalworking was also an important economic factor in the Sauerland and Bergisches Land (the region of North Rhine-Westphalia between the Rhine, Sieg and Ruhr rivers) where, for hundreds of years, mills and forges had harnessed the water power of the many brooks and streams in the valleys. However, all this changed with the advent of modern industrialisation. Businesses expanded and the population grew rapidly, both being equally dependent on ever-increasing demand for water which could no longer be provided by traditional pumping stations.

this sparked off a typhus epidemic in Gelsenkirchen in 1901 caused by poor water quality in the mains supply. The river was just able to meet the demands without help until the end of the 19th century although during some summers, when there was below-average rainfall, a catastrophic water shortage prevailed in the lower reaches of the Ruhr. It was only when the quantities extracted shot up within a few years from 90 million cubic metres (1893) to 135 million cubic metres (1897) and then to more than 500 million cubic metres, that the natural supply proved insufficient. The demands on the water reserves were so great they could no longer be guaranteed without recourse to large-scale engineering solutions in the form of dams. With the help of the cities of Altena and Gevelsberg, the first two dams in the drainage basin of the Ruhr, the Fuelbecke [3] and Heilenbecker [4], with a storage capacity of 7 million cubic metres and 4.5 million cubic metres respectively, were built in 1896 to supply local drinking water.

However, the thirst of the Ruhrgebiet seemed insatiable and on December 10, 1899 the Ruhrtalsperrenverein (Ruhr Valley Dams Association) was established with the stated aim 'to improve the water level of the River Ruhr in terms of quantity and composition by the furthering of dam building in the drainage basin of the river'. Generous subsidies were made available by the Association to support small dam-building co-operatives, and in 1904 dams in the valleys of the Hasper [5], Fürwigge [6], Glör [7] and Ennepe [8] were officially opened providing a combined volume of 16.1 million cubic metres. All four were built according to plans drawn up by Professor Intze.

The setting up of the Ruhr Valley Dams Association, involving the water extraction companies and those using the river to power machinery, was originally voluntary, but given a legal framework in 1913 with the passing of the Ruhr Valley Dams Legislation. This law made it possible to levy financial contributions from all those involved in the water industry. Because of the pressing need for more water, the Ruhr Valley Dams Association had already (in 1906) decided on a major project, the Möhne dam [9]. This, with its initial reservoir capacity of some 135 million cubic metres, far exceeded what had

The Sorpe was Germany's largest earthen dam. The concrete core — the backbone of the dam — is shown under construction. When completed in 1935 it reached a height of 69 metres.

The Ennepe, some 12 kilometres east of Wuppertal was built between 1902-04, this picture showing the 'heaven's ladder' method of construction. The dam wall was raised by 10 metres in 1912 which increased the capacity to 12.6 million cubic metres of water.

The industrial revolution led to new technical developments in the construction of reservoirs. This in turn prompted some cities to plan their own reservoirs for the storage of drinking water. The great pioneer of German dam building was Dr. Ing. Otto Intze, Professor at the University of Technology at Aachen. In 1891, and without building permission, the city of Remscheid, 30 kilometres east of Düsseldorf, completed Germany's first dam in the Eschbach valley [1] to provide a reservoir for drinking water. Professor Intze employed the latest civil engineering techniques when he drew up his plans for the dam wall and he kept the local government in Düsseldorf informed of the progress of the works. However, the authorities were reluctant to accept responsibility for the dam's ability to withstand the pressure of water and, as a result, building permission was withheld, yet the dam was completed and the authorities presented with a fait accompli.

Remscheid's success spurred on the neighbouring town of Lennep to build a dam of its own and Professor Intze and Albert Schmidt, a local chartered building engineer, paved the way for the project. The Panzertalsperre [2] had just been completed when building permission came through! It was not long before other reservoirs were constructed in the Bergisches Land — a region which can truly be considered as the birthplace of modern dam building — and soon a multiplicity of artificial lakes appeared around the River Wupper. However, the reputation of the Bergisches Land was soon to be challenged by the Sauerland.

The second half of the 19th century saw a sharp growth of industry and population in this region between the Rivers Emscher and Ruhr. Within a few decades, a predominantly agricultural area had been transformed into the 'Ruhrgebiet' which, with its coal and steel reserves, was to become the centre of heavy industry in Germany. In order to supply the rapidly expanding cities and their factories with sufficient water, the river that gave its name to the region was run dry. Pumping stations in the Ruhr valley sprouted like mushrooms. Scant consideration was paid to the problem created by over-extraction and

By far the largest reservoir in Germany — the Eder — was built between 1908 and 1914.

hitherto been the conceived limits for such constructions in Europe. The dam wall of granite masonry blocks stretched across a 650-metre-wide bend in the valley and rose 37.3 metres above its floor. The foundations did not simply extend down to the bedrock but were excavated a further three metres in order to prevent any movement of the wall due to water pressure. The total height was therefore 40.3 metres to the crest with a width of 34.2 metres at the base, the thickness of the wall at its crown being 6.25 metres. Construction began in 1908 and was completed in 1912. (It was officially opened on July 12, 1913.)

Fifteen kilometres south-west from the Möhne stands the Sorpe dam [10] forming — when completed in 1935 — the second biggest reservoir in the Sauerland. In contrast to the Möhne, the Sorpe was constructed with an earth embankment comprising rubble and an inner concrete core. The dam came into service in 1935 and consists of 3.25 million cubic metres of rubble and 130,000 cubic metres of concrete. For many years the 69-metre-high Sorpe was Germany's highest earthen dam, surmounted by a crest 700 metres long and ten metres wide. With its capacity of 70 million cubic metres, the Sorpe dam forms a reservoir with sufficient resources to supplement the others in the drainage basin of the Ruhr during the so-called 'double dry years'. (The latter term describes the situation when the rainfall is below average for two consecutive years and when the other reservoirs are unable to meet the needs of the Ruhrgebiet.) It also has another special feature — a 'one-year plus reserve'. This means that its reservoir has a capacity greater than the annual average of waters entering from the drainage basin. As a result, water flowing into the Sorpe must be carefully husbanded as it takes a long time to be replenished. In the 1950s, the ingress of water was increased further by means of additional channels from neighbouring river valleys, yet the amount of electricity generated at the Möhne and Sorpe dams is insignificant in terms of other hydro-electric plants.

Some 70 kilometres south-east of the Möhne, lies the Eder dam [11]. This was built thanks to Prussian legislation passed in 1905, the content of which included a law relating to the planning and construction of the Mittelland Canal designed to link the River Elbe

Kaiser Wilhelm II inspects the construction work on the Eder dam in August 1912.

with the Rhine. The stated aim was 'to improve the rural economy, reduce flood damage and construct a network of inland waterways'. The western section of the canal as far as Hanover was completed first, and to ensure it had sufficient water, guaranteed quantities had to be drawn from the River Weser throughout the year, but without endangering navigation on that river. This required the building of dams in the area where waters fed the Weser. So came about the construction of the gigantic (at the time) Eder reservoir (1908-14) with a capacity of 202 million cubic metres and the Diemel dam [12] (1912-24) with a capacity of 20 million cubic metres.

The Eder dam, a slim construction with no clay apron at the front, is eight metres higher than the Möhne. Although the wall of the Eder is 200 metres shorter, it nevertheless holds back an additional 70 million cubic metres of water. Another reason for the creation of the 27-kilometre-long Eder reservoir was to provide protection against flooding, since the Eder had shown itself to be the most turbulent river in the Hessen region. Floods in 1840, 1881 and 1890 had caused great destruction, but in future the waters were to be captured within the Eder reservoir and stored for use during dry periods. The difference in water levels would also be exploited for the generation of electricity at power stations situated at the dam itself and also at the end of the stilling basin which serves as the lower basin for the Waldeck 1 power station.

Other dams serving the Ruhrgebiet are the Lister (1912) [13] of 22 million cubic metres; the Henne (1905) [14] with 11 million cubic metres; the Kerspe (1912) [15] comprising 15.5 million cubic metres; Jubach (1906) [16] of just over one million cubic metres; the Bever (1898 and 1939) [17] of 27 million cubic metres; the Neye (1909) [18] of 6 million cubic metres, and the Oester (1906) [19] of 3 million cubic metres. (By comparison, the pre-war US Boulder Dam, renamed Hoover Dam in 1947, completed in 1936 has a reservoir capacity of 38,547 million cubic metres. One of the largest dams existing today — the Kariba in Zimbabwe — holds 180 billion cubic metres of water — 1,400 times as large as the Möhne reservoir.)

Air Attacks on Reservoirs and Dams

As early as September 1937, the RAF had prepared detailed intelligence reports on the largest German dams. The preferred targets of the Air Staff were the armament factories of the Ruhr — the heart of the German defence industry — with the associated waterways of the River Weser and the Mittelland Canal along which war materials would be transported. If the dams could be destroyed, at a stroke the Ruhr would be drained of water and the hydro-electric power stations put out of action.

The following year, with the Second World War looming, the 18th meeting of the Bombing Committee was convened at the Air Ministry at Adastral House, Kingsway, on July 26, 1938, the topic under discussion being 'Air Attacks on Reservoirs and Dams'.

The prevailing view had always been that targets of this nature would be extremely difficult to attack from the air and that any such attacks would be uneconomical. For this reason the importance and far-reaching consequences of a successful strike on specific dams within the territory of potential enemies had thus far not been fully appreciated, and these targets did not figure in the current edition of the Manual of Air Tactics.

Air Vice-Marshal W. Sholto Douglas, the Assistant Chief of the Air Staff, chaired the meeting and opened the debate saying that recent investigations had indicated that certain reservoirs in Germany and Italy formed what might be termed an 'Achilles heel' in those countries in that their industrial power system was based on power derived almost entirely from these sources. He said that it was the object of the meeting 'to enquire into the extent to which effective air action against the dams of the reservoirs and similar targets would be possible'.

The information currently available was briefly summarised and circulated as Bombing Committee Paper No. 16. This described the types of construction and siting of the dams, notes on the potentialities of different weapons of attack, and also on the probability of hitting such targets by high-altitude bombing.

The minutes record that Squadron Leader C. G. Burge, representing the Air Targets Sub-Committee of Air Intelligence, reported that 'the amount of water consumed in the whole of Germany was only three times that of the Ruhr' and that 'the bulk of it was obtained from one large reservoir contained by a single-arch dam known as the Möhne dam'. He added: 'There were also four or five other reservoirs in Germany which fed the inland waterways. The destruction of these dams, he was informed, would leave the waterways high and dry and, as water transport figured very largely in the German transportation system, the extra traffic thrown on the roads and railways would very soon tend to cause chaotic conditions. The recent drought had caused several of these reservoirs to dry up, and the whole of two or three large stretches of waterways were inactive for three or four weeks, thus throwing a very heavy burden on the railways.'

Squadron Leader Burge mentioned that at a recent meeting of the Air Ministry Transportation Targets Committee, Mr Hawkins, an expert on dam construction, had strongly recommended an attack on the lower face as being the best method, the end in view being to fracture the structure, when it was considered that the pressure of the water would probably do the rest.

Dr R. Ferguson of the Research Department at Woolwich agreed that 'if a semi-armour-piercing bomb could be used to attack the target almost normal to its surface with sufficient striking velocity, that the bomb, when inside the target, would do immense damage'. He considered however, that some sort of specially-designed propelled bomb would be necessary in order to obtain the required velocity at low altitudes. He said that it was known that a 500lb semi-armour-piercing bomb, when propelled, had penetrated five feet into the concrete. The thickness of the dam at a depth of 40 feet was approximately 12 feet. If a bomb could be driven into the wall to a depth of five feet, the remaining seven feet should be severely damaged, and the damage thus obtained would be immeasurably greater than that caused by an ordinary bomb, fused for delayed-action, which detonated on the surface of the target.

Group Captain Norman Bottomley of Bomber Command enquired which would have the greater effect — a bomb of 1,000lbs detonated under water on the high water side, or a similar bomb a short distance on the low water side of the structure. Dr Ferguson

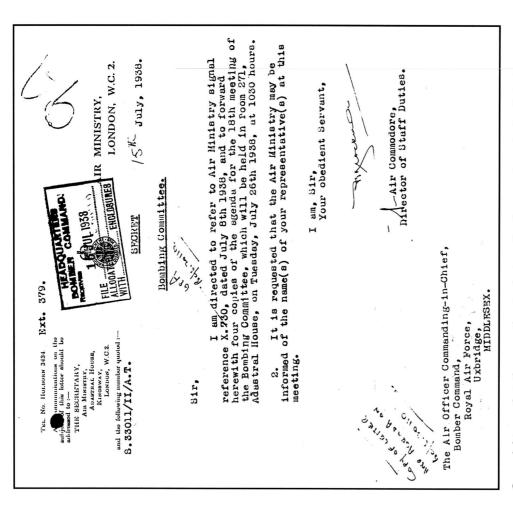

One might say that the operation to destroy the German dams in the Ruhr began on Tuesday, July 26, 1938 at a meeting chaired by Air Vice-Marshal W. Sholto Douglas, the Assistant Chief of the Air Staff. The Air Ministry was represented by Air Commodore R. P. Willcock, Group Captain A. Gray, Wing Commander H. V. Rowley, Wing Commander C. P. Brown, Wing Commander L. F. Pendred, Squadron Leader J. D. F. Bruce, Squadron Leader C. G. Burge and Mr R. Struthers and Mr E. M. Lake. Group Captain N. H. Bottomley, Group Captain J. F. Summers and Squadron Leader L. V. B. Bennett represented Bomber Command with Wing Commander G. H. Boyce present for Coastal Command. Group Captain R. B. G. Neville represented No. 25 (Arm) Group and Wing Commander W. R. Cox No. 1 Air Armament School. The Research Department at Woolwich was represented by Wing Commander F. R. Alford and Dr R. Ferguson, while Major R. Purves and Squadron Leader J. L. Wingate were present from the Royal Aircraft Establishment at Farnborough. The Admiralty representative was Lieutenant-Commander V. W. L. Proctor with Colonel I. Simpson for the War Office. The Air Ministry secretary was Flight Lieutenant F. G. Brockman.

Group Captain Bottomley enquired whether there were many dams in this country of the types which had been discussed, which an enemy could attack in the same way and, if so, were any defensive measures being taken? It was stated that there were several large reservoirs in Wales feeding Birmingham and Liverpool but no one at the meeting could voice an opinion as to what defensive measures were being contemplated.

At the end of the discussion the Committee were of opinion that the destruction of reservoir dams through the medium of attack from the air would, with certain qualifications, be a feasible operation. It was considered that low-level or low-dive attacks on these targets were the most likely to be successful, and were the most desirable from the operational point of view.

'The committee concluded that 'the single-arch dam is the most likely type upon which attack will be required and the weapons recommended, on the basis of existing information (in order of priority), are: (a) a number of 18-inch torpedoes; (b) large general-purpose bombs; (c) 500lb general-purpose bombs; (d) 500lb anti-submarine bombs'.

The chances of success with options (c) and (d) were considered to be less favourable than with (a) and (b), but in the event of an emergency in the immediate future, it might be found that 500lb GP, and anti-submarine bombs were the only weapons available for immediate use.

Finally, the meeting reported that 'at the present time, it is considered that the attack should be directed primarily against the high water side of the dam. Attack against the lower side is considered less likely to be effective unless a bomb can be devised which will develop sufficient striking velocity to achieve the necessary amount of damage at low altitudes.'

Historic Kingsway, carved out of a slum area in London's West End at the end of the 19th century, where Adastral House, with the wireless masts on its roof, the new headquarters of the Royal Air Force, was opened at its southern end in 1919. Room 271 was the scene of the historic meeting in 1938 to examine the possibilities of destroying the German dams.

replied that a bomb fused with a short delay dropped on the high water side would be the most effective, but he pointed out that a bomb with a high charge-to-weight ratio would be necessary, and that it would have to fall very close to the wall. Wing Commander H. V. Rowley of the Air Ministry remarked that the only large bomb which was now available was the 2,000lb armour-piercing which had a very small charge-weight ratio and would therefore be practically useless for the purpose. As general-purpose bombs of 1,000 to 2,000lbs in weight would not be available for some time, and the largest bomb then available was only of 500lb, consequently he felt inclined to favour the torpedo as being the most suitable weapon for attack from the high water side.

Major R. Purves of the Royal Aircraft Establishment stated that the standard 18-inch torpedo had a range of 1,500 yards, and could be set to run between 5 and 45 feet below the water. The weight of the explosive in the warhead was just under 400lbs. If dropped 300 or 400 yards from the face of the dam it would reach the correct depth. It could be fitted with a net-cutter which was so efficient that ships had now abandoned the net system of protection.

Squadron Leader Burge then suggested that the element of uncertainty as to the outcome of the attack could be reduced by attacking on both sides of the dam, with bombs and/or torpedoes. This would give a double chance of success. In this connection Dr Ferguson said that the 500lb anti-submarine bomb already in service, which had a charge-weight ratio of 55 per cent and which could be carried in any bomber, would be better than a 500lb general-purpose bomb when dropped on the high water side. It would, however, break up in the event of a direct hit on the wall.

It was ironic that almost exactly six years later — on Friday, June 30, 1944 — the Germans came to within an ace of achieving retribution with a direct hit on the building. In the third worst V1 incident to befall London, a flying bomb struck the road just 40 yards in front of the entrance to Adastral House, completely demolishing the ten-foot-high blast wall in front of the entrance and killing 48, the majority of the 200 casualties being passers-by.

At the same time, a series of experiments to determine the amount of explosive necessary to destroy a dam began in October 1940 at the Road Research Laboratory at Harmondsworth, which was directed by Dr William Glanville. The RRL had been heavily involved with military matters since the outbreak of the war and had considerable experience in building models for predicting explosions and their effect. Dr Glanville discussed these problems in detail with Wallis and agreed — it would appear completely off the record — to initiate a series of tests on various model dams. He put together a team under Dr A. R. Collins and gave the responsibility for measuring the effects on the models to one of his scientific advisors, Mr D. G. Charlesworth.

The basis of these experiments was very simple. The scaled-down models were constructed of a similar material to those in Germany (and one in Sardinia) and these were subjected to relatively smaller amounts of explosive so that they would behave in the same way as the originals. Dr Collins explains how they went about it.

'Sir Reginald Strading, Chief Scientific Adviser to the Ministry of Home Security, who had a connection with Wallis through Professor A. J. S. Pippard, discovered that there was a small, unused concrete gravity dam in the Elan Valley water supply system of the City of Birmingham which was available for tests with explosives and he wrote to the corporation accepting responsibility on behalf of the Ministry for any costs that might be incurred.

'It had also been established that a model would reproduce accurately the effects of an explosion on a structure if the same materials were used and all the linear dimensions, including those of the explosive, were reduced by the same ratio. This rule, however, applied only to the effects caused directly by the explosion and a model would not necessarily represent the final effects on the structure as a whole because these would depend also on the type of structure, the site and the extent of the direct damage and the existing static loads including those due to gravity.

A wartime aerial view of the Road Research Laboratory at Harmondsworth. It was here that test explosions were carried out on scale models of the Möhne dam and of the Nant-y-Gro dam at Rhayader in Wales which had been secured for large-scale tests once the experiments on the models had been conducted. The area used for the testing can be seen top right.

Dr Barnes Wallis — the inventor of the bouncing bombs — photographed after the war in his office at Burhill, Walton-on-Thames, where his theory about the bombs took shape. A large photograph of the Möhne dam hangs on the wall (see page 169). Sir Barnes Wallis died on October 30, 1979 at the age of 92 having been knighted for his war services in 1968.

Barnes Wallis Goes to War

When war broke out Barnes Wallis was assistant chief designer of Vickers-Armstrong's Aviation Section at Weybridge. Here, quite independently of the Air Ministry, he concerned himself with how the energy sources of the Axis powers, Germany and Italy, might be eliminated. Specialist publications provided him with the necessary background information on the German dams, and he was firmly of the opinion that knocking out the water reserves of the Ruhr would severely curtail steel production for the German armament industry as the production of each tonne of steel required 100 tonnes of water. Articles in publications such as *Zeitschrift für die gesamte Wasserwirtschaft*, 'Journal for the National Hydro Economy) *Zeitschrift für Bauwesen* in the *Schweizerische Wasserwirtschaft* (Building Construction in the Swiss Hydro Economy) and *Das Gas- und Wasserfach* (Gas and Water Industry) showed Wallis the technical minutiae of the German reservoirs.

By the end of 1940 Wallis believed that a heavy bomb dropped from 40,000 feet and weighing 10 tons would penetrate deep into the soil around the dams and that shock waves to the foundations would bring about the collapse of the whole structure. (Wallis was able to realise this idea in 1945 when his 10-ton 'Grand Slam' bombs were employed to destroy U-Boat bunkers and railway viaducts.) However, back in 1940, there was neither the 'earthquake bomb' nor an aircraft large enough to deliver and drop it accurately. Consequently, the Air Ministry did not attach a great deal of importance to the theory of the big bomb, believing that technical considerations made the proposal impossible to carry out. Nevertheless, from August 1940, Wallis managed to test streamlined model bombs in a wind tunnel at Teddington.

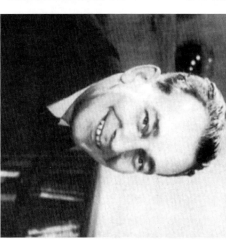

Left: The Director of the Road Research Laboratory was Dr W. H. Glanville. Right: Dr A. R. Collins oversaw the tests for Barnes Wallis and discovered by chance that a relatively small explosive charge, if placed in direct contact with the wall, would cause it to collapse.

Two models (above) of the Nant-y-Gro dam were built to the scale of 1:10 for experiments before two tests were carried out on the actual dam in Wales to prove the theory in practice.

'In many instances the final results could be deduced easily but, in the case of a gravity dam which depended on its own weight for stability, the reliability of a model test was uncertain because gravity could not be scaled. It was, nevertheless, hoped that some means of circumventing this problem might be found and, in the first week of October 1940, Wallis visited the RRL and discussed plans for the research with Dr Glanville, Dr A. H. Davis (Assistant Director at the Laboratory) and myself. Without indicating how the choice had been made, Wallis suggested that the three main targets should be the Möhne and Eder masonry gravity dams in Germany and the Santa Chiara di Ula multiple-arch dam on the Tirso River in Sardinia. Of these dams Tirso was much the most vulnerable and, as it was not attacked, it can be dealt with very briefly, though the experimental work occupied several months. The maximum thickness of the reinforced concrete arches was only about five feet and preliminary tests on sections of concrete pipe indicated that a charge of about 3000lb of explosive would be likely to breach at least one of the arches if it were detonated in the water up to about 50ft away. This was confirmed by tests on an accurate 1:25 scale model built at the Building Research Station which showed also that a contact charge of about only a few hundred pounds might well be effective and that an attack with anti-submarine bombs or torpedoes would be possible.

'The problems posed by the Möhne and Eder dams were much more formidable. Both dams were massive structures built of cyclopean masonry and inherently stable even when cracked. The apparent impossibility of making allowance for the effects of gravity in a test on a model also added a major uncertainty. Of the two dams, Eder was the higher, but Möhne was the more conservatively designed and had a clay bank reaching almost to mid-height on the water face. It was therefore decided to use Möhne as the prototype for both dams, to confine the model to the centre section between two

11

towers which were at approximately the third points of both dams, and to make it on a linear scale of 1:50. In view of the absence of previous experience and the uncertainty about the effects of gravity, it was also decided to make the model as accurately as possible by using a scaled-down form of masonry composed of mortar blocks 0.4 × 0.3 × 0.2 inches in size, and to lay them in the curved courses used in the prototype. This proved to be a tedious task requiring the production and laying by hand of some five million blocks which Dr Norman Davey and his colleague at the Building Research Station, Mr A. J. Newman, offered to undertake. The model was built on a small stream in the grounds of the Station.

'Wallis had estimated that his proposed ten-ton bomb would contain about seven tons of explosive and, on a scale of 1:50, this was represented by two ounces. He also suggested that, in a high-altitude attack by a squadron of aircraft, it could be expected that one bomb would fall in the reservoir within about 150ft of the dam. These parameters were, therefore, adopted as convenient starting points in the tests and preliminary experiments, using short lengths of concrete with a cross-section similar to that of the model, indicated that the effect would be significant but not so great as to prevent further tests.

'The true-to-scale model was fitted with a simple gauge to measure the horizontal deflection at mid-height at the centre, and the first charge of 2oz of gelignite was fired in the reservoir 3ft from the dam. The result was a short horizontal crack just below the crest and a vertical crack through the whole cross-section at the centre. The test was witnessed by several members of the Committee and it was agreed that the damage, if reproduced on the full scale, would require immediate repairs and perhaps a reduction in water level, but it could not be regarded as being enough to warrant an attack. The test was, therefore, repeated but this caused little more damage. Three more tests were made at the same distance of three feet, three at a distance of two feet, and, finally, two were made at a distance of one foot. Each of these caused a little more damage and the final effect was quite substantial. It was considered that, on the full scale, the same damage would require the

A deflective gauge was installed to record vibrations of the wall caused by underwater explosions at varying distances.

Above: To try to replicate the construction of the Möhne as near as possible, millions of tiny blocks were used to build the first test model at the Building Research Station at Garston near Watford. *Below:* For later models (in 1:50 scale), this time-consuming process was abandoned in favour of using mortar spread in ayers.

12

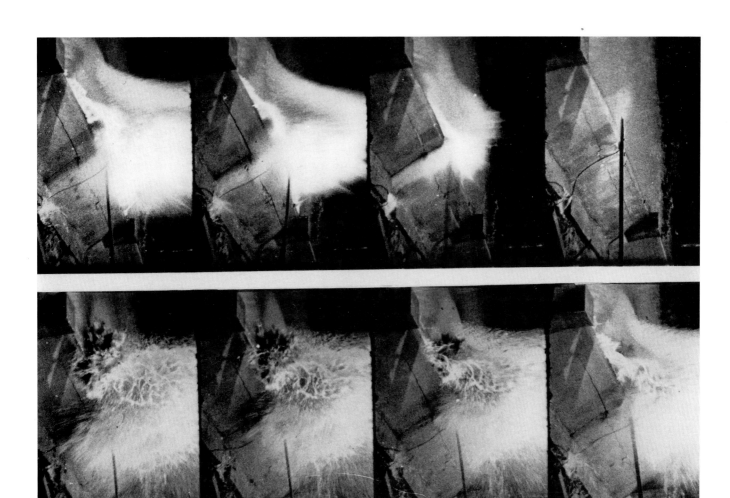

Left: Slow motion cine footage shows the effects of two different experimental explosions on the model of the Möhne. The aim of the research was to establish the relationship between weight of explosive and the distance from the wall at which blasts became effective, depending on the varying water level in the reservoirs. *Above and below:* **Author Helmuth Euler found the old model — which cost the princely sum of £34 13s to build — still standing at Garston.**

13

made on some new models of Möhne and it was found that a one-ounce charge of PE at a distance of one foot caused significantly more damage than that achieved in the earlier tests with gelignite. Although the damage was still insufficient to warrant an attack with bombs dropped in the reservoir, the Committee felt that little further progress could be made without some information on the effects of scale and that the risks in making a test on the Elan Valley dam had to be accepted.

'The dam had been built at the turn of the century on a small stream, called the Nant-y-Gro on the bank of the Caban Coch Reservoir, to provide water for the construction of the main dam. It was made of mass concrete and was 30ft high at the centre, 180ft long, straight in plan and with a height/thickness ratio of 1.5 to 1.0. The reservoir was only 250ft long and any water released as a result of the test would flow safely into the main reservoir. A survey was made of the construction joints and cracks in the dam and the contours of the bed of the reservoir. Two models of the dam and reservoir complete with cracks and joints were then made at the laboratory and tested with one-ounce charges of PE at distances ranging from 6 inches to 24 inches and at depths of 18 inches and 24 inches.

'The results showed that the straight dam behaved in a way that was rather different from that seen in the Möhne models. There was no rebound effect resulting in forward movement, but there was evidence of a form of vertical 'bending' in which the blocks between the construction joints tilted away from the explosion and then fell back into place.

'Of this series of tests, that in which the charge was 9 inches from the dam and 18 inches deep produced enough damage to allow a comparison to be made, but not so much as to prevent another test on the Nant-y-Gro dam if required. The test was therefore repeated on the Nant-y-Gro dam with the ten-times equivalents of 62.5lb of TNT fired 7.5ft from the dam at a depth of 15 feet. The damage in both structures consisted mostly of cracking along the construction joints but some parts of the spillway walls were detached as a result of the reflected tensile stress forecast by Wallis but, as none of the effects would have been affected by gravity, they gave no indication of any way in which an allowance could be made for this factor.

'A solution to the problem was, however, found almost by chance shortly afterwards. Although Wallis had suggested to Tizard a direct hit on the water face of the dam, during the early stages of the investigation, he had rejected it in his paper to the Air Ministry and apparently agreed with the Committee that the idea was impracticable. Soon after the first test on the Nant-y-Gro dam, however the research team had to demolish a damaged model and decided to do this with a contact charge. The effect was unexpectedly severe and some parts of the model were projected more than 20ft downstream. When Glanville saw this result he reacted with a proposal for a means of allowing for the effect of gravity. He argued that as both the mass of the dam and the energy of the explosive varied with the cube of the scale, the distance travelled by any fragment of the structure would be the same irrespective of the scale. He therefore suggested that if the distance travelled by every fragment were reduced in proportion to the scale ratio, the model would then represent what would occur on the full scale. The model was, therefore, reconstructed in this way and the result was a realistic breach.

'Further tests on new models were then made with one-ounce contact charges at depths of 9 and 12 inches and with 4 and 8oz charges at a depth of 12 inches. After reconstruction of the models the results showed that a 4oz charge at a depth of 12 inches produced an adequate breach, and the Committee decided to reproduce this test on the Nant-y-Gro dam with the ten-times equivalent weight of explosive of 280lbs, provided by a 500lb anti-submarine bomb, at a depth of 10ft. The result was a breach 60ft wide and 24ft deep which was rather less wide and deeper than that forecast from the model, but was regarded as being more realistic and more reliable than the result with the tenth-scale model. It was, of course, not possible to reconstruct the Nant-y-Gro dam to represent the result on larger scales, but from the positions of the fragments it was deduced that an increase in scale of up to about five times would have little effect on the relative dimensions of the breach.'

'While these tests were taking place, Wallis was preparing a long paper entitled *A Note on the Method of Attacking the Axis Powers*, the product of a year-long intensive period of thought, research and experimentation. It was finalised in March 1941 and some 100 copies were circulated in military and political circles, the outcome being the formation of a committee — the Aerial Attack on Dams Committee — to progress the matter further.

Following the model testing, in May 1942 the Nant-y-Gro dam at Rhayader was prepared for large-scale experiments.

reservoir to be drained and closer examination showed that the damage was more extensive than it appeared to be on the surface. The tests, however, represented a very heavy and extremely accurate attack that was very unlikely to be achieved in practice and it was therefore decided to continue with the investigation.

'It was, however, impracticable to construct more models by the time-consuming process used in making the first and the research team therefore devised a simpler method of representing the masonry construct on by layers of mortar formed by a sliding template which allowed a model to be made in two weeks instead of the three months required by the original process. A test made to compare the two processes showed that while there were some differences in the behaviour of the models they were not important in comparison with other uncertainties.

'The BRS model had, however, been built on clay soil while the Möhne and Eder dams were founded on rock. The next test was therefore made to examine this factor with a new model built on an existing massive block of concrete. The results were, however, little different and it seemed at this time that there was only a remote possibility that a large gravity dam could be breached by the method proposed by Wallis. The Air Ministry, therefore, suggested that an attack might be made using a number of bombs or mines fitted with pressure-activated fuses which could be detonated by the shock wave from a normal bomb dropped further away from the dam so that the individual shock waves would amalgamate. Charlesworth investigated this proposal but found that the pressure-activated fuses would have to operate within one millisecond and this was regarded as being impracticable at the time.

'There was, however, a more promising development towards the end of 1941 when new and more powerful explosives were procured and one of these, plastic explosive (PE), was made available to the laboratory. After preliminary experiments, tests were

14

In general, the tests on the models had been disappointing and the first explosion on the real Nant-y-Gro dam shown here failed to breach the wall. Dr Collins thereby concluded that it would take in excess of 13 tons of explosive to be effective against the Möhne and of course no such bomb, or aircraft to carry it, then existed. However, this discouraging result was overturned when Collins set out to see what the charge would do if set off in contact with the face of the model dam at Harmondsworth. When he tested his theory, he was

astonished to see how easily the model wall was breached by just 2oz of explosive with mortar flying 20 feet away. So a second test was ordered in Wales using a 500lb naval mine containing a scaled-up charge of 280lbs of explosive. This was suspended at the mid-point of the dam below the surface of the water and detonated on July 24. The result astounded those watching, indicating that 7,500lbs of explosive, if set off in contact with the Möhne dam wall, would breach it.

3. Möhne Dam

(a) Although the precise nature of the catastrophe which would overtake the Ruhr valley as the result of the release of the greater part of the contents of this dam in the space of a few hours cannot be estimated in advance, it is agreed that there is every prospect that both the physical and the moral effects of the flood which would be produced are likely to be sufficiently great to justify this operation in themselves, even if there were no other significant effects.

(b) The destruction of this dam would not necessarily have any large or immediate effect on the supply of industrial and household water in the Ruhr area. This immediate source of the greater part of the Ruhr water supply is the underground water-bearing strata, supplemented by colliery water, water pumped back from the Rhine and water drawn from the Emscher river and canal systems. The purpose of the system of storage dams of which the Möhne dam is largest, is the conservation of rainfall, by means of which the level of the underground water can be maintained and protected from permanent depletion. In an emergency, a large and possibly adequate volume of water supplies might be obtainable for some months by drawing heavily on these underground supplies and depleting their level. Whether or not such depletion would proceed at a rate or reach the stage where economies in water consumption would have to be introduced would depend upon the amount of rainfall, the speed of repairs to damaged conservation works and the efficacy of emergency measures to obtain additional water (e.g. from the Rhine). If these factors were all unfavourable, a difficult situation might well develop by the end of the summer, but it is not possible to state that a critical shortage of water supplies in the Ruhr would be a certain and inevitable result of the destruction of the Möhne dam.

The model-making section at RAF Medmenham — the complex in Oxfordshire which housed the RAF's photo-reconnaissance interpretation unit — constructed models of the Möhne (above), Eder and Sorpe reservoirs to the scale of 1:6000. On the morning of the raid three large boxes were unsealed at RAF Scampton and the targets revealed to the assembled aircrews. The models have been held by the Imperial War Museum in London since 1946.

In preparing this report on the economic and moral consequences of the destruction of the German dams, the Ministry of Economic Warfare set out the pros and cons of each of the main targets. They also put forward the Lister, Ennepe and Henne as other possibilities and mentioned that there were another seven smaller dams within the Ruhr catchment area although the Möhne and Sorpe between them held 75 per cent of the total reservoir capacity. The Eder was the odd man out, seen here in profile via the model which was built in 1:40 scale in about 1910. Helmuth Euler discovered that it still stands off the northern shoreline near the Nieder-Werbe—Waldeck road (see map page 72). Normally submerged, the model was photographed one autumn when the water level had fallen sufficiently to expose it.

The Targets

On March 28, 1943, the RAF's Air Staff once again considered the targets in Germany and clarified the economic effect and the effect on morale of destroying the Möhne dam. At the same time they considered the increased impact if the Sorpe and Eder were to be simultaneously destroyed. This is their report drawn up on April 2, 1943.

ECONOMIC AND MORAL CONSEQUENCES OF THE DESTRUCTION OF GERMAN DAMS

Introduction

1. This memorandum assesses the probable economic and moral consequences of the destruction of the Möhne dam and the added effects which could be expected from the destruction of the Sorpe and Eder dams.

2. It has been prepared in consultation with the Scientific Advisers to the Minister of Production and with reference to the statements attributed to them in the introduction to the Combined Operations dossier on the Möhne dam. The latter document, on certain points of detail, over-states the expectations of the Scientific Advisers as to the probable economic effects and the following conclusions should be taken as representing their actual views.